Learning and Teaching Languages Through Content

Language Learning and Language Teaching

The *LL&LT* monograph series publishes monographs as well as edited volumes on applied and methodological issues in the field of language pedagogy. The focus of the series is on subjects such as classroom discourse and interaction; language diversity in educational settings; bilingual education; language testing and language assessment; teaching methods and teaching performance; learning trajectories in second language acquisition; and written language learning in educational settings.

Series editors

Nina Spada
Ontario Institute for Studies in Education, University of Toronto

Jan H. Hulstijn
Department of Second Language Acquisition, University of Amsterdam

Volume 18

Learning and Teaching Languages Through Content
A counterbalanced approach
by Roy Lyster

Learning and Teaching Languages Through Content

A counterbalanced approach

Roy Lyster

McGill University

John Benjamins Publishing Company

Amsterdam / Philadelphia

™ The paper used in this publication meets the minimum requirements
of American National Standard for Information Sciences – Permanence
of Paper for Printed Library Materials, ANSI z39.48-1984.

Library of Congress Cataloging-in-Publication Data

Roy Lyster
    Learning and teaching languages through content : a counterbalanced
        approach / Roy Lyster.
        p.   cm. (Language Learning and Language Teaching, ISSN 1569–9471
; v. 18)
    Includes bibliographical references.
        1. Language and languages--Study and teaching. I. Title.

    P51.L97 2007
    407.1--dc22   2007004379
    ISBN 978 90 272 1974 9 (Hb; alk. paper)
    ISBN 978 90 272 1976 3 (Pb; alk. paper)

John Benjamins Publishing Co. · P.O. Box 36224 · 1020 ME Amsterdam · The Netherlands
John Benjamins North America · P.O. Box 27519 · Philadelphia PA 19118-0519 · USA

For Bertha, George, and James

Table of contents

Tables and figures

Preface

This book is intended for graduate courses in Applied Linguistics and Second Language Acquisition or for advanced levels of undergraduate teacher education programs. I hope also that practicing teachers will read the book as a source of professional development, as well as other educators, curriculum designers, and administrators working in a variety of second language instructional settings, whether content-based or not. While the book aims to enable educators in immersion and content-based classrooms to consider ways of integrating more focus on language, I hope as well that it will inspire educators in traditional language classrooms to consider integrating more content-based instruction as a means of enriching classroom discourse.

I am indebted to the many immersion teachers who have generously opened their classroom doors to me over the past several years: Brigitte Besner, France Bourassa, Todd Chowan, Steven Colpitts, Maureen Curran-Dorsano, Patrice Delage, Al Delparte, Martine Delsemme, Patricia Donovan, Réna Gravel, Linda Hadida, Madeleine Hall, Susan Hawker, Claude Hébert, Marita Heikkinen, Chris Holden, Maurice Kalfon, Claude Karsenti, Tom Konicek, Claude Leroux, Carole Lidstone, Marie-Josée Messier, Nicole Rosconi, Asher Roth, Luce Turgeon, Suzanne Ujvari, André Vachon, Normand Veilleux, Josiane Waksberg, Marie Whabba, and Keisha Young. This book is dedicated to these and other teachers working in the forefront of what continues to be considered by many as an "experiment" in bilingual education. The prerequisite for working in the context of educational innovation is a tremendous amount of dedication, and the consequence is a huge amount of preparation that at times might go unnoticed, but at other times is hopefully the source of much professional as well as personal satisfaction.

Many publications helped to fill gaps in my knowledge and to extend my awareness of an entire spectrum of immersion and content-based classrooms. In particular, volumes by Bernhardt (1992), Cloud, Genesee, and Hamayan (2000), Day and Shapson (1996), Genesee (1987), Harley, Cummins, Swain, and Allen (1990), and Johnson and Swain (1997) all proved to be invaluable sources of information. In addition, I acknowledge the significant influence of Birgit Harley's seminal work on the interlanguage development of learners exposed to content-based instruction, as well as Merrill Swain's work on the instructional limitations of content-based approaches. Special thanks go to Hirohide Mori for discussions about the role of counterbalance in content-based instruction and to Leila Ranta for discussions about the role of awareness, practice, and feedback.

I express my heartfelt thanks to Fred Genesee, Nina Spada, and Merrill Swain for providing helpful feedback on this book. For comments on specific chapters, I thank Iliana Panova and Leila Ranta, as well as Ingrid Veilleux and her study group of immersion teachers in Richmond, BC: Brooke Douglas, Lisa Dar Woon Chang, Natalie Wakefield, Kim Leiske, Diane Tijman. Thanks also to Kees Vaes, Acquisition Editor at John Benjamins, for his continued support, patience, and efficiency. Finally, I gratefully acknowledge the financial support provided by the Social Sciences and Humanities Research Council of Canada (grants 410-2002-0988, 410-98-0175, 410-94-0783) and the *Fonds pour la formation de chercheurs et l'aide à la recherche* (grant 97-NC-1409) to conduct some of the classroom-based studies referred to throughout this book.

Roy Lyster
Montreal, January 2007

CHAPTER 1

Introduction

This book draws on findings from classroom-based research to paint a portrait of second language pedagogy consisting of instructional options that enable learners to engage with language through content. The term 'content-based instruction' is used broadly throughout this book to encompass classrooms where subject matter is used at least some of the time as a means for providing second language learners with enriched opportunities for processing and negotiating the target language through content. The research on which this book draws derives for the most part from immersion classrooms, because of the vast array of studies conducted in immersion settings over the past 40 years. Wesche (2002) estimated that research on immersion has been documented in "several thousand reports to school boards, articles, book chapters, masters and doctoral theses, and books" (p. 357). Many studies have served specifically as program evaluations whereas others have been more process-oriented investigations that contribute to the field of applied linguistics in ways that are relevant to both theory and practice. An underlying assumption in this book is that there is still room for improvement in immersion and other content-based second language programs. Its aim is to explore, both theoretically and practically, a range of pedagogical possibilities for tackling some of the challenges inherent in teaching languages through content, so that students will be in a better position to reap the benefits of content-based second language instruction.

As the social and linguistic demographics of today's schools continue to evolve at remarkable speed, reflecting similar changes around the globe, one can predict a continued need to develop more effective second language programs to meet the changing needs of local communities. To develop such programs, good reasons abound in support of teaching additional languages through content rather than through traditional methods. In a nutshell, Snow, Met, and Genesee (1989) argued that, whereas language development and cognitive development go hand-in-hand for young children, traditional methods tend to separate language development from general cognitive development. Typically, traditional methods isolate the target language from any substantive content except for the mechanical workings of the language itself, whereas content-based instruction aims to integrate language and cognitive development. Content-based instruction provides not only the cognitive basis for language learning, however, but also the requisite motivational basis for purposeful communication. Lightbown and Spada (2006) referred to content-based and immersion programs as the "two for one" approach, because learners in these programs learn subject matter and the target language at the same time, thus significantly increasing their exposure to the target language. More instructional time in a second or foreign language is otherwise difficult to allocate in a school curriculum already full to capacity.

It is hoped that potential readers not directly involved in immersion or other content-based instructional settings will recognize potential implications for other second language classroom settings, as identified by Genesee (1991) and addressed throughout this book: namely, that second language instruction in any setting can increase its effectiveness by (a) integrating content other than only language itself, (b) incorporating ample opportunities for interaction in classroom activities, and (c) planning systematically for language development. Much research in applied linguistics continues to explore the corollary upshot of content-based instruction, investigating how learners can effectively and systematically engage with language in classrooms that emphasize content-driven input, purposeful tasks, and meaning-focused interaction. This book aims to enable educators in meaning-based classrooms to consider ways of integrating more focus on language, and those in traditional language classrooms to consider integrating more content-based instruction as a means of enriching classroom discourse.

1.   Emphasizing language in content-based instruction

Reporting on a celebration of 40 years of immersion on Montreal's south shore, Peritz (2006) described this parent-driven initiative as follows: "Like many groundbreaking ideas, it began simply enough – in this case, in a suburban living room near Montreal. It was October, 1963, and a group of forward-thinking parents had a radical proposal." The idea of implementing a home-school language switch for majority-language children so that their early education would be primarily in their second language was certainly a radical change in St. Lambert, Quebec, in the 1960s. Education theorists with critical views of schooling grounded in a range of epistemological perspectives (e.g., Giroux 1992; Kohn 1999), however, might not consider an educational initiative aiming to maintain the overall status quo of schooling and its curriculum, apart from a language switch, to be so "groundbreaking," "forward-thinking," and "radical."

The perspective taken in this book is that immersion and other content-based programs have far-reaching potential to innovate, but they have not yet necessarily reached their full potential. As for any educational initiative, immersion and content-based programs need to continue to evolve in ways that (a) respond to the needs of changing student populations and their communities; (b) incorporate relevant research findings about effective instructional practices; and (c) adopt instructional practices that situate teachers in a more interactive relationship with students and knowledge than do transmission models of teaching (see Smith & Shapson 1999). Content-based instruction and its theoretical underpinnings are conveniently consistent with current educational thought that attributes considerable importance to language as a cognitive tool in all learning. For this reason, content-based programs have considerable potential, not only for developing high levels of bilingual proficiency among a wide range of learners, but also for creating ideal conditions for both language and cognitive development – given optimal instructional practices that nurture the relationship between language development and content learning. The perspective adopted throughout this book is that instructional practices designed to foster continued second language growth through immersion and content-based approaches were initially formulated rather tentatively (see Chapter 2) and thus underlie attested shortcomings that characterize students' second language proficiency. Specifically, initial conceptualizations of immersion and content-based instruction underestimated the extent to which the target language needs to be attended to.

With respect to emphasizing language in immersion and content-based instruction, different instructional practices now abound and, as one would thus expect, second language learning outcomes differ from one classroom to the next. To help explain discrepant findings across classroom-based studies, Lyster and Mori (2006) proposed the *counterbalance hypothesis*, which states that:

> Instructional activities and interactional feedback that act as a counterbalance to the predominant communicative orientation of a given classroom setting will be more facilitative of interlanguage restructuring than instructional activities and interactional feedback that are congruent with the predominant communicative orientation. (p. 294)

Counterbalanced instruction will be invoked throughout this book as a principled means for systematically integrating content-based and form-focused instructional options. A counterbalanced approach to content-based instruction supports continued second language development by orienting learners in the direction opposite to that which their classroom environment has accustomed them. According to the counterbalance hypothesis, instruction that requires learners to vary their attentional focus between, on the one hand, the content to which they usually attend in classroom discourse and, on the other, target language features that are not otherwise attended to, facilitates the destabilization of interlanguage forms. The effort required for learners to shift their attention to language form in a meaning-oriented context is predicted to leave traces in memory that are sufficiently accessible to affect the underlying system. The genesis and rationale for counterbalanced instruction will be further expounded in Chapter 5.

The classroom-based research reported throughout this book indicates unequivocally that the extent to which content-based teaching is language-rich and discourse-rich clearly affects second language learning outcomes. A powerful example of differential teacher effectiveness comes to us from Joan Netten's large-scale study of 23 immersion classrooms ranging from Grades 1 to 3 in the Canadian province of Newfoundland (Netten 1991; Netten & Spain 1989). Classroom observations and teacher interviews revealed major differences between two of the classrooms (A and C), in spite of a common curriculum. In Classroom A, lecture and drills comprised only 3% of instructional time; 13% of class time was devoted to teacher-student interaction following a question/answer format, 15% was devoted to group work and discussion, and 27% was devoted to seat work with the teacher assisting individual students. In Classroom C, lecture-type instruction and drill-type activities together comprised 35% of instructional time; 18% of class time was devoted to seatwork, and only 4% to group work and discussion. The teacher of Classroom A used non-verbal comprehension aids only minimally; instead, she used verbal messages to facilitate comprehension of the target language. In Classroom C, almost 90% of comprehension aids used by the teacher were either visual (pictures, drawings) or paralinguistic (gestures, body language). Students in Classroom A made regular use of the second language to express themselves about academic and social matters to the teacher and to each other. Students in Classroom C spent half of their time in activities in which they listened to or produced formulaic responses. The teacher of Classroom A tended to provide explicit correction, whereas the main correction technique in Classroom C involved recasting – "echoing techniques" whereby "the incorrect response of a pupil was quietly restated in its correct form" (Netten 1990: 301; see Chapter 4 for examples of recasts).

To assess their overall scholastic ability, students' were given the Canadian Cognitive Abilities Test (CCAT). To assess students' achievement in the second language, the *Test diagnostique de lecture* (Tourond 1982) was used. In comparison to the CCAT scores of all other classrooms in the province, Classroom A had the lowest relative ability, while that of Classroom C was moderately high. Yet, the results on the measure of second language achievement showed that Classroom A was among the best in the province, whereas Classroom C attained generally low results relative to its high CCAT scores. Netten and Spain (1989) concluded, "Despite a common curriculum, teachers organize and instruct their classes differently, and these differences are significant with respect to the learning outcome for pupils" (p. 499).

Of particular interest is the unexpected and striking finding that a low-ability class excelled in their second language achievement in comparison to a high-ability class that demonstrated low second language achievement. The researchers attributed this remarkable achievement on the part of Classroom A to the instructional practices they observed in that classroom and which differed from those in Classroom C. The more effective instructional options included:

— more teacher-student interaction
— more opportunities for meaningful interaction among peers
— less reliance on non-verbal clues to convey meaning
— more explicit than implicit correction

Teachers who orchestrate opportunities for students to engage with language in this way are more apt than others to succeed in moving their students' second language development forward. Day and Shapson (1996) concluded in a similar way that instructional practices that emphasize discourse and the use of language as an instrument for learning have much to contribute to improving the second language learning environment in immersion classes. They observed marked differences in instructional strategies employed by immersion teachers during science lessons. In one science classroom, students were seen "as a community of learners engaged in discourse about science" (p. 80), while in another the limitations of traditional pedagogy were more evident as the teacher "repeated or rephrased what [students] said, wrote the answers on the board, and had students take notes" (p. 56). Genesee (1987) as well argued that more discourse-rich approaches are needed for immersion programs to fulfill their potential, but acknowledged that "many immersion programs, and indeed many regular school programs, do not do this" (p. 77). Such an approach requires a great deal of systematic planning and does not necessarily come naturally to content-based teachers. At the interface of content and language teaching are challenging obstacles that prevent content teaching from being ipso facto good language teaching (Swain 1985, 1988).

Obstacles may have in part derived from uncertainty surrounding the importance attributable to second language learning and teaching in immersion and content-based instruction. Is language learning a primary or secondary goal? Genesee (1994a) argued that "language learning in immersion is secondary to academic achievement" (p. 2). Met (1998), however, suggested that, in content-driven immersion programs, "student mastery of content may share equal importance with the development of language proficiency" (p. 40). In keeping with Allen et al. (1990:75) who state that, in immersion, "language and content learning are equally important goals," the perspective taken in this book is that second language learning and academic achievement are inextricably linked and thus share equal status in terms of educational objectives. If second language learning were not a primary goal of immersion and content-based instruction, then it would be much easier for children to engage with the school curriculum entirely through their first language. To justify the extra effort required of all stakeholders associated with programs promoting curricular instruction in more than one language, including teachers and students alike, learning the additional language needs to be a primary objective.

2.   Characteristics and contexts of content-based instruction

Content-based approaches are known to come in many different shapes and sizes. Met (1998) described a range of content-based instructional settings along a continuum varying from content-driven language programs, such as total and partial immersion, to language-driven content programs, which include language classes either based on thematic units or with frequent use of content for language practice. Towards the middle of the continuum are program models in which students study one or two subjects in the target language along with a more traditional language class. Still others refer to sheltered content instruction (Echevarria & Graves 1998), sustained content teaching (Pally 2000), theme-based and adjunct language instruction (see Brinton, Snow, & Wesche 1989), and, in many European contexts, content and language integrated learning or CLIL (Marsh, Maljers, & Hartiala 2001). Cloud, Genesee, and Hamayan (2000) used the term 'enriched education' to refer to school programs that integrate bilingual proficiency as a full-fledged objective along with other curricular objectives. Enriched education includes second and foreign language immersion programs as well as two-way immersion programs, which normally integrate a similar number of children from two different mother-tongue backgrounds (i.e., Spanish and English in the US) and provide curricular instruction in both languages (Lindholm-Leary 2001). Also included under the rubric of enriched education are developmental bilingual education programs, designed for language-minority students in the US who receive at least half of their instruction through their primary language throughout elementary school.

Content-based programs have the requisite flexibility to meet the needs and wishes of local communities, with variations in grade-level entry point, target languages, and academic subjects associated with each target language. In Montreal, for instance, where the first early total immersion program began in 1965, as many as 43 programmatic variations have since been identified (Rebuffot 1998). An example of programmatic variation is *double immersion*, which uses, in addition to English, two non-native languages for curricular instruction, such as the French-Hebrew immersion program for English-speaking children in Montreal (Genesee 1998). Internationally, immersion programs have also been adapted increasingly to meet local educational needs for teaching various languages. Edited volumes by Johnson and Swain (1997) and Christian and Genesee (2001) provide excellent sources of information about immersion and other types of bilingual education programs in a range of international contexts.

Educational instruction that entails a home-school language switch is far from new. It can be traced back as early as 3000 BC to Sumer where speakers of Akkadian, in order to become scribes, learned Sumerian and its cuneiform method of writing by studying subjects such as theology, botany, zoology, mathematics, and geography through the medium of Sumerian (Germain 1993). Comparable practices of adopting a written variety as the medium of instruction to the exclusion of the home vernacular have tended to be the rule rather than the exception in the history of education: for example, Latin in Western Europe until a few hundred years ago and classical Arabic in Muslim countries today (Swain & Johnson 1997). Likewise, Western imperial powers imposed their languages on colonies so that a language such as English, French, Dutch, Portuguese, or Spanish became the medium of instruction in schools not only for the colonizers but also for certain social classes of the colonized. Today, many children continue to experience a home-school language switch because their home language, which may or may not have its own standard written form, lacks majority status and/or prestige in the community. Contexts where individual minority-language students find themselves without any first language support and with a majority of native speakers of the target language are regarded as 'submersion' classrooms. In contrast, 'immersion' is a form of bilingual education that aims for additive bilingualism by providing students with a sheltered classroom environment in which they receive at least half of their subject-matter instruction through the medium of a language that they are learning as a second, foreign, heritage, or indigenous language. In addition, they receive some instruction through the medium of a shared primary language, which normally has majority status in the community.

The term 'immersion' has been used since the first half of the 20th century to refer to highly intensive language classes involving second language study, usually for several hours a day and several weeks at a time (Ouellet 1990), a connotation still associated with the term 'immersion' in the promotional campaigns of many private language schools. The term has been used as well to refer to situations in which second language learners immerse themselves in the target language and culture, usually temporarily and often as they work or study, by going to live in the target community (Swain & Johnson 1997). In the field of applied linguistics, however, the more recent sense of the term 'immersion', as used by Lambert and Tucker (1972) to describe their study of a groundbreaking experiment in bilingual education that began in 1965, is now well established. English-speaking parents in St. Lambert, a suburb of Montreal in Quebec, Canada, were concerned that the traditional second language teaching methods that prevailed at the time would not enable their children to develop sufficient levels of proficiency in French to compete for jobs in a province where French was soon to be adopted as the sole official language. Parents had reservations about enrolling their children in schools for native speakers of French, and the latter were reluctant to admit large numbers of English-speaking children. Consequently, parents developed instead what came to be known as an early total immersion program.

Lambert and Tucker's (1972) seminal study of this "early immersion" initiative examined two groups of English-speaking children who were taught exclusively through the medium of French in kindergarten and Grade 1 and then mainly in French (except for two half-hour daily periods of English language arts) in Grades 2, 3, and 4. The widely disseminated results were positive with respect to the children's language development in both English and French, as well as their academic achievement and affective development. Other immersion programs spread quickly in the Montreal area, then across Canada and were modified in some contexts to include alternative entry points and variable proportions of first and second language instruction (Rebuffot 1993). Immersion programs have since been developed to teach various languages in a wide range of contexts around the world (Johnson & Swain 1997).

Swain and Johnson (1997) identified key features that define a prototypical immersion program. In a prototypical program, students' exposure to the second language tends to be restricted to the classroom where it serves as a medium for subject-matter instruction, the content of which parallels the local curriculum. Immersion teachers are typically bilingual; students enter with similar (and limited) levels of second language proficiency; and the program aims for additive bilingualism. Students in immersion classrooms usually share as their main language of communication a majority language that is used socially, administratively, and academically: socially with peers both inside and outside the school; administratively by the school to communicate with parents and even with students; and academically as a medium of instruction, increasingly so as students advance through higher grade levels. More recently, Swain and Lapkin (2005) updated these prototypical features to reflect increasing changes in urban demographics whereby (a) immersion students no longer necessarily share the same first language and (b) the target language can no longer be accurately referred to as the second language for many students, who increasingly represent culturally diverse and multilingual school populations. Throughout this book, the terms 'second language' and 'target language' are used interchangeably.

One strand of immersion education includes programs that have been designed to promote the learning of a second or foreign language, with or without official status:

- English immersion in Japan (Bostwick 2001a, 2001b), Hong Kong (Johnson 1997), Singapore (Lim, Gan, & Sharpe 1997), Korea (Lee 2006), Germany (Burmeister & Daniel 2002), and South Africa (Nuttall & Langhan 1997)
- French immersion in Canada (Genesee 1987; Rebuffot 1993)
- Swedish immersion in Finland (Björklund 1997)
- Estonian immersion for Russian-speaking students in Estonia (Genesee 2004:550)
- Immersion in English, Russian, German, French, Italian, and Spanish in Hungary (Duff 1997:23)
- Immersion in French, German, Italian, Japanese, Chinese, and Indonesian in Australia (Johnson & Swain 1997:18)
- Immersion in Spanish, French, Japanese, Chinese, and German in the US (Met & Lorenz 1997:243)
- Catalan immersion in Spain (Artigal 1991, 1997)
- Basque immersion in Spain (Arzamendi & Genesee 1997)

– Irish immersion in Ireland (Hickey 2001)
– Welsh immersion in Wales (Baker 1993)

Another strand of immersion education includes programs that have been designed for the purpose of maintaining heritage or indigenous languages:

– German immersion in Alsace (Bange 2005; Petit 2002)
– Ukrainian immersion in Canada (Lamont, Penner, Blower, Mosychuk, & Jones 1978)
– Korean immersion in Japan (Cary 2001)
– Hebrew immersion (along with French, i.e., double immersion) in Canada (Genesee & Lambert 1983)
– Mohawk immersion in Canada (Jacobs & Cross 2001)
– Maori immersion in New Zealand (Benton 2001)
– Hawaiian immersion in the US (Slaughter 1997; Yamauchi & Wilhelm 2001)

These examples are illustrative, but not exhaustive, of the extent to which immersion has become associated with an increasingly wide range of contexts. Moreover, immersion programs are evolving in ways that blur borders between the two strands. For example, Basque-medium schools in the Basque Country were originally created as a language maintenance program for native speakers of Basque, but are now regarded "as both total immersion programs for native Spanish-speaking students and first language maintenance programs for native Basque speakers" (Cenoz 1998). Catalan immersion programs in Catalonia were designed for native speakers of Spanish but, for a school to be designated as an immersion school, as many as 30% of its students can have Catalan as their family language (Artigal 1997). In some cases, therefore, use of the term 'immersion' depends on which students in any given classroom one is referring to. For example, in the case of Wales, Baker (1993) writes: "The kaleidoscopic variety of bilingual educational practice in Wales makes the production of a simple typology inherently dangerous. ... A Welsh-medium school usually contains a mixture of first language Welsh pupils, relatively fluent second language Welsh speakers, plus those whose out-of-school language is English (i.e., 'immersion' pupils)" (p. 15; see Hickey 2001, for a similar description of Irish-medium education in Ireland). Even in St. Lambert, Quebec, where the first Canadian French immersion program began in 1965 with homogenous groups of English-speaking children, the student population has drastically changed: 38% of its elementary students now claim French as their home language; only 53% claim English and 9% claim another language (Hobbs & Nasso-Maselli 2005).

3.   Research on outcomes of immersion education

Immersion programs tend to be housed in *dual-track schools*: that is, schools that offer both an immersion and a regular non-immersion program. Although evaluation studies recorded higher second language proficiency levels for students enrolled in *immersion centres* (i.e., schools that offer only the immersion program; see Lapkin, Andrew, Harley, Swain, & Kamin 1981), dual-track schools continue to be the norm. More typically, immersion programs are classified according to: (a) the proportion of instruction through the first language relative to instruction through the second language and (b) the grade level at which the program begins. In *total immersion*, 100% of the curriculum is taught through the second language; the immersion is likely to be total, however, for only two or three years because some instruction in the first language is eventually introduced. In *partial immersion*, a minimum of 50% of the curriculum is taught in the second language for one or more years (Genesee 1987, 2004). Program comparisons indicate that early total immersion programs yield better results than early partial immersion programs.

With respect to entry points, typical immersion programs tend to be classified according to three types. *Early immersion* begins at kindergarten or Grade 1 (age 5 or 6) and normally involves, in the case of total immersion, the teaching of literacy skills first in the second language, followed by the introduction of instruction in first language literacy in Grades 2 or 3. In the case of early partial immersion, literacy training tends to occur simultaneously in both languages from Grade 1 on. *Middle immersion* begins at Grades 4 or 5 (age 9 or 10) and *late immersion* begins at Grades 6, 7, or 8 (age 11, 12, or 13). Middle and late immersion programs thus include students who are already schooled in first language literacy and have usually been exposed to some instruction in the second language as a regular subject. In addition, *post-secondary immersion* programs provide sheltered classes for university students studying a subject such as psychology through the second language (Burger & Chrétien 2001; Burger, Wesche, & Migneron 1997). The most popular program in Canada, Finland, Spain, and the US is the early total immersion option.

Overall, early immersion students tend to develop higher levels of second language proficiency in comparison to middle or late immersion students, although the differences are not as great as one might expect. Advantages have been found for early immersion students on measures of listening ability and fluency in oral production (Turnbull, Lapkin, Hart, & Swain 1998). Students from middle and late immersion programs may catch up with early immersion students in writing tasks and other measures requiring knowledge of formal language features. Some studies have shown that differences between early and late immersion students disappear altogether at the university level, although these findings need to be interpreted with caution, because late immersion programs attract a self-selected, academically successful group that may easily catch up with early immersion students during secondary school (Turnbull et al. 1998; Wesche 1993). For this reason, early immersion has been considered to be a more accessible option for a wider range of students. Genesee (2004) proposed, with respect to comparisons of early and late starting points, that outcomes co-vary with multiple factors such as overall quality of instruction more so than actual starting point. For example, a late immersion program with results below par is the English-medium program implemented in Hong Kong secondary schools for native speakers of Cantonese (Johnson 1997; Marsh, Hau, & Kong 2000). Wesche (2002) suggested that the program's disappointing outcomes in both target language and content learning demonstrate "the hazards of universal application of late immersion, particularly in a situation in which the first and second languages are very different, learners enter the program with inadequate second language (English) proficiency to support English-medium instruction, curricular and pedagogical adaptation is not possible, and teachers themselves may not fully master the instructional language" (p. 370).

3.1 First language development and academic achievement

Early evaluation studies of immersion programs (Genesee 1987; Lambert & Tucker 1972; Swain & Lapkin 1982) yielded consistent and positive results with respect to first language development and academic achievement; these results have recently been substantiated by Turnbull, Lapkin, and Hart (2001). The academic achievement of immersion students in subjects they study through the second language is equivalent to that of non-immersion students studying the same subjects in their first language, and their first language development ranges from equivalent to superior to that of non-immersion students. Similarly, Genesee (1992) found that students with learner characteristics that are disadvantageous with respect to academic and linguistic abilities demonstrate the same levels of first language development and academic achievement as similarly disadvantaged students in non-immersion programs (see Genesee

2006, for an overview of this research). In the case of two-way immersion, English speakers tend to outscore Spanish speakers on English-language measures while being outperformed by Spanish speakers on measures in Spanish (Howard, Christian, & Genesee 2004).

3.2 Social-psychological outcomes

Social-psychological studies comparing immersion and non-immersion students demonstrated that immersion students develop additive as opposed to subtractive bilingualism; that is, their perceptions of their cultural identity and their sense of ethnic group membership are as positive as those of non-immersion students (Genesee 1987). These studies also revealed that, in comparison to non-immersion students, immersion students perceive less social distance between themselves and native speakers, and develop more positive attitudes towards the second language and its native speakers. However, this trend is short-lived, being more consistently documented with younger than with older students and early in students' participation in the program but diminishing with each grade level. Similar results have been found in two-way immersion programs (Genesee & Gándara 1999).

Although many French immersion students in the Canadian context remain geographically remote from the target community, this is not the case in Montreal and Ottawa where studies have been able to compare immersion and non-immersion students with respect to second language use outside the classroom. In comparison to non-immersion students, immersion students in Montreal reported that they were (a) more comfortable and confident when using the second language with native speakers, (b) more likely to respond in the second language when addressed in the second language, and (c) less likely to avoid situations in which the second language was spoken. However, immersion students were not more likely than non-immersion students to actively seek opportunities for second language exposure by watching television, listening to the radio, or reading books in the second language (Genesee 1987). Wesche (1993) found a similar type of "reactive use" of the immersion language among immersion graduates in the Ottawa area. She also reported that graduates of immersion programs featuring contact with native speakers tended in their young adult lives to use the second language on social occasions and with neighbours, and to attend plays performed in the second language. Graduates of immersion programs that included access to the target language through activities outside the classroom reported having more positive attitudes toward using the target language and also higher levels of current use of the target language for reading and at work. Immersion graduates attending an English-speaking university in a unilingual anglophone community in Nova Scotia expressed significantly higher levels of willingness to communicate and frequency of communication in their second language than non-immersion graduates (MacIntyre, Baker, Clément, & Donovan 2003).

3.3 Second language outcomes

Research has clearly demonstrated that immersion students, regardless of program type, develop much higher levels of second language proficiency than do non-immersion students studying the second language as a regular subject (i.e., for one period per school day). This is equally true of immersion students with learner characteristics that are disadvantageous with respect to academic and linguistic abilities: They achieve higher levels of second language proficiency than non-immersion students with similar disadvantages studying the second language as a regular subject (Genesee 1992). In comparison to non-immersion students, immersion students develop (a) almost nativelike comprehension skills as measured by tests of listening and reading comprehension; and (b) high levels of fluency and confidence in using the second language, with production skills considered non-nativelike in terms of grammatical accuracy, lexical variety, and sociolinguistic appropriateness (Harley et al. 1990). In the case of two-way immersion, Spanish speakers develop increasingly balanced oral and written proficiencies in both languages, whereas English speakers continue to perform better in English than in Spanish (Howard, Christian, & Genesee 2004).

This section elaborates on the second language proficiency of immersion students with reference to Canale and Swain's (1980) well-known model of communicative competence (see also Bachman 1990). Their model reflected advances in the sociology of language and a move away from the more narrowly defined construct of linguistic competence (Chomsky 1965). Following Hymes (1971) and Gumperz (1972), who defined communicative competence as the ability to vary language in accordance with social context and to select grammatically correct forms that appropriately reflect social norms, Canale and Swain (1980) and Canale (1983) identified four interrelated components underlying communicative competence:

– grammatical competence:

  – knowledge of the second language code and skill in using it

- sociolinguistic competence:

    - ability to recognize and produce the second language in accordance with socially appropriate norms

- discourse competence:

    - ability to understand and produce second language discourse in a cohesive and coherent manner

- strategic competence:

    - ability to employ strategies to sustain communication in spite of gaps in second language communicative ability

Harley et al. (1990) conducted a large-scale study of the second language proficiency of immersion students, operationalizing proficiency in terms of grammatical, sociolinguistic, and discourse traits. In comparison to native speakers of French of the same age (i.e., 11–12 years old), immersion students performed as well on measures of discourse competence, but "were clearly less proficient on most grammar variables, and especially on verbs in the oral grammar test" (p. 16). They also performed significantly differently on all sociolinguistic measures. Specifically, immersion students used significantly fewer instances of singular *vous* and conditional verb forms to express politeness. With respect to strategic competence, prior research had confirmed that immersion students were highly successful at using communication strategies enabling them to get their message across through recourse to their first language and the use of gestures, general all-purpose terms, or circumlocutions (Harley 1984).

With respect to lexical variety, Harley (1992) documented a tendency for immersion students to use a restricted vocabulary limited to domains experienced in school, and to overuse simple high-coverage verbs at the expense of morphologically or syntactically complex verbs, such as pronominal and derived verbs. Allen et al. (1990) found generally that immersion students' first language significantly influenced their second language lexical proficiency (see Jiang 2000). Other studies of the interlanguage development of immersion students revealed non-targetlike uses of grammatical and sociolinguistic features that include, but are not limited to, the following:

- prepositions (Harley et al. 1990)
- object pronouns (Harley 1980)
- word order (Selinker, Swain, & Dumas 1975)

- grammatical gender (Harley 1979, 1998; Lyster 2004a)
- features of the verb system such as the use of imperfective aspect, conditionals, and third-person agreement rules (Harley 1986)
- productive use of derivational morphology (Harley & King 1989)
- use of verbs with syntactic frames incongruent with the learner's first language (Harley 1992)
- singular *vous* and mitigating conditionals (Harley et al. 1990; Lyster 1994; Swain & Lapkin 1990)
- vernacular features and other informal variants (Mougeon & Rehner 2001; Rehner & Mougeon 1999)

What emerges from these studies is that immersion students are second language speakers who are relatively fluent and effective communicators, but non-targetlike in terms of grammatical structure and non-idiomatic in their lexical choices and pragmatic expression – in comparison to native speakers of the same age. Day and Shapson (1996) suggested, however, that "we may want to have different standards in certain areas of communicative competence than those attained by native-speakers of the language" (p. 98). They argued that immersion students have "no strong social incentive to develop further toward native-speaker norms" (p. 95) because of their success in communicating with one another and with the teacher.

Immersion students tend indeed to learn an academic register of the target language, without acquiring colloquial lexical variants that might otherwise facilitate more authentic communication among peers (Auger 2002; Tarone & Swain 1995). Tarone and Swain (1995) described immersion classrooms as diglossic settings in which the second language represents the superordinate or formal language style while the students' first language represents the subordinate or vernacular language style. As the need to use a vernacular becomes increasingly important to pre-adolescents and adolescents for communicating among themselves, they use their first language to do so since they are familiar with its vernacular variants. The second language remains the language of academic discourse and not for social interaction among peers. This observation may parallel the finding that immersion students perceive increasingly more social distance between themselves and native speakers of the immersion language as they progress through the program (Genesee 1987). The influence of peers in the immersion classroom is so strong that Caldas (2006) reported that children being raised bilingually (French/English) in Louisiana, with one or even two francophone parents at home, develop English accents and adopt English word order in their use of French as a result of their participation in French immersion. Not surprisingly, when French immersion students have the opportunity to interact with native speakers of French of the same age, for example on a school exchange, they often encounter difficulties in making themselves understood (MacFarlane 2001; Warden, Lapkin, Swain, & Hart 1995).

The second language learned by students in French immersion has been criticized for lacking cultural relevance and social utility (e.g., Bibeau 1982; Singh 1986). Calvé (1986) argued that immersion education results in a linguistic code used more as a communication tool than as a language imbued with social relevance and steeped in cultural values. Lyster (1987) also questioned the social value of immersion students' tendency for "speaking immersion" – a classroom code generally understood by classmates and their teacher – but argued that it was the result of ill-defined pedagogical strategies and inappropriate instructional materials designed for native speakers of the target language rather than for second language learners. Also questioning the appropriateness of instructional materials used in French immersion classrooms, Auger (2002; see also Nadasdi, Mougeon, & Rehner 2005) reported anecdotally that immersion graduates living and working in the bilingual city of Montreal felt "frustration at trying to use, in real-life settings, the language that they had spent so many years learning in school," and, even with respect to receptive skills, "difficulty understanding what coworkers would say to them" (p. 83).

Genesee (1994a) described the productive skills of immersion students as "linguistically truncated, albeit functionally effective" (p. 5), but also stressed that immersion students' second language proficiency does not limit their academic development: "The documented effectiveness of the immersion programs indicates that an approach in which second language instruction is integrated with academic instruction is an effective way to teach the language skills needed for educational purposes" (Genesee 1987:176). But would it also be possible for immersion students to develop a wider range of skills to enable them to use the second language for social purposes, with some degree of communicative effectiveness, as well as for educational purposes? Such would be more in keeping with the overall objectives of Canadian and other immersion and content-based programs which, in addition to ensuring normal first language development and academic achievement, aim to develop functional competence in both speaking and writing the target language, as well as an understanding and appreciation of target language speakers and their culture (Genesee 1987; Met 1994; Rebuffot 1993).

4.   Theoretical perspectives

Content-based instructional approaches to second language learning and teaching generally draw support from a range of theoretical perspectives. As Echevarria and Graves (1998) stated in reference to sheltered content classrooms, "effective teachers typically use a balanced approach that includes choices rooted in different learning theories" (p. 36). The theoretical perspective adopted throughout this book attributes complementary roles to both cognition and social interaction in the learning enterprise, and thus draws on a socio-cognitive view of second and foreign language learning. Advocating a similar perspective, Bange (2005) brings together Anderson's work on information processing and Bruner's work on scaffolded interaction in a coherent fashion that underscores the complementarity of these perspectives and their potential to drive a pedagogical approach that creates optimal conditions for learning both language and content in classroom settings. Incorporating Bruner's (1971) argument that "growth of mind is always growth assisted from the outside" (p. 52) and the corollary view that "mental processes are as social as they are individual and as external as they are internal" (Block 2003:93), a socio-cognitive view of learning applies aptly to school settings, where "learning is a social as well as a cognitive process, one influenced by the relationships between student and teacher and among students" (August & Hakuta 1997:85).

Cognitive theory provides a helpful framework for understanding second language development in classroom settings and especially the developmental plateaus reportedly attained by immersion students. Cognitive theory draws on information-processing models to describe second language learning as the acquisition of complex cognitive skills, involving the interrelated development of (a) mental representations stored in memory and (b) processing mechanisms to access these representations. Many researchers have drawn on cognitive theory to explain second language learning and use (e.g., Bange 2005; de Bot 1996; DeKeyser 1998, 2001, 2007; Hulstijn 1990; Johnson 1996; Lyster 1994a, 2004a; McLaughlin 1987, 1990; McLaughlin & Heredia 1996; O'Malley & Chamot 1990; Ranta & Lyster 2007; Towell & Hawkins 1994).

Anderson (1983, 1985) described skill acquisition as a gradual change in knowledge from declarative to procedural mental representations. Declarative knowledge entails knowing concepts, propositions, and schemata, including static information such as historical or geographical facts encoded in memory. Procedural knowledge is knowledge about how to do things. This involves the ability to apply rule-based knowledge to cognitive operations, such as solving problems or following steps toward an end goal, and to motor operations, such as those required to ride a bicycle or to use a typewriter (Anderson 1983). With respect to language, declarative knowledge refers to knowledge of language items and subsystems, such as word definitions and rules, whereas procedural knowledge involves language processing, including online comprehension and production through access to representations stored in memory.

The transformation of declarative knowledge into procedural knowledge involves a transition from controlled processing, which requires a great deal of attention and use of short-term memory, to automatic processing, which operates on automatised procedures stored in long-term memory (Shiffrin & Schneider 1977). The transition from controlled to more automatic processing results from repeated practice in transforming declarative representations into production rules in contexts clearly linking form with meaning (DeKeyser 1998). The proceduralisation of rule-based declarative representations occurs through practice and feedback (Anderson, Corbett, Koedinger, & Pelletier 1995), which together move learners towards a restructuring of interlanguage representations, enabling them to access a better organized representational system (McLaughlin 1990; Skehan 1998). DeKeyser (2007) argued that "a high degree of automaticity, however hard it may be to achieve, is the ultimate goal for most learners, both because of its impact on the quality of linguistic output and because of how it frees up resources for processing message content instead of language" (p. 288). Segalowitz (2003) cautioned, however, that empirical research has not yet yielded "a tidy picture whereby learning grammatical structure proceeds simply from knowledge of examples to automatized (proceduralized) rules [or] from the effortful application of rules to the retrieval of memorized instances" (p. 400). He invoked instead an integration of rule-based and exemplar-based processes (see also Skehan 1998), which will be taken up further in Chapter 3 with regard to production practice.

Yet another cognitive perspective is Bialystok's (1994) model comprising two related yet distinct processing components: analysis and control. The process of analysis concerns the rearrangement of mental representations "loosely organized around meanings" into "explicit representations that are organized around formal structures" (p. 159). The process of control involves choices "about where attention should best be spent in the limited-capacity system" and is thus crucial for developing automaticity. In this view, learning does not proceed from explicit representations of declarative knowledge, but rather from increasingly explicit representations of implicitly acquired and unanalyzed knowledge. In the case of young learners exposed to subject matter through a second language, their knowledge of the target language in the initial stages is largely implicit and composed of unanalyzed chunks. They benefit, therefore, from instruction designed to increase analysis of mental representations because, according to Bialystok, this will lead to an increase in accessibility to knowledge and also supports the development of literacy skills. In contrast, "Knowledge of language represented in a less analyzed form will limit the learner in the range of functions that can be achieved" (p. 160).

Skill-acquisition theory has proven useful for understanding interlanguage development and apparent plateau effects in immersion and content-based classrooms. In the absence of feedback or other types of appropriate instructional intervention, interlanguage representations can also become automatized procedures stored in long-term memory. Johnson (1996) pointed out that "naturalistic" approaches to language teaching, such as immersion, are designed to bypass the initial development of declarative knowledge and serve instead to directly develop procedural encodings of the target language. He argued that encodings that come into the system in an already proceduralized form "quickly become highly automatized and impermeable to change" (p. 99; see also McLaughlin 1987). The early emphasis on language use in most immersion and content-based programs encourages the deployment of procedures that operate on linguistic knowledge which has not yet been acquired in the target language, thus necessitating recourse to other mental representations such as knowledge of first language structures. From this perspective, the challenge for teachers is twofold: to help students develop declarative knowledge from the procedural knowledge that they acquired in a more or less naturalistic way (Johnson 1996), and to push students to develop new target-like representations that compete with more easily accessible interlanguage forms (Ranta & Lyster 2007).

Bange (2005) argued that, in second or foreign language teaching, there has been a tendency for instruction to be considered sufficient even if it aims only to develop declarative knowledge, without proceeding to the next step of providing opportunities for students to proceduralize their declarative knowledge. He also identified an obvious challenge in this regard: Procedural knowledge is acquired through action (i.e., learning by doing; see Bruner 1971), so learners are expected, paradoxically, to accomplish actions they have not yet acquired. He argued that the solution to the paradox lies in social interaction and, more specifically, in Bruner's notion of scaffolding between expert and novice, which "enables a child or novice to solve a problem, carry out a task or achieve a goal which would be beyond his unassisted efforts" (Wood, Bruner, & Ross 1976: 90). Taking on the mentoring role, teachers promote the appropriation of new knowledge as they provide the amount of assistance that students need until they are able to function independently. According to Bruner (1977),

> There is a vast amount of skilled activity required of a 'teacher' to get a learner to discover on his own – scaffolding the task in a way that assures that only those parts of the task within the child's reach are left unresolved, and knowing what elements of a solution the child will recognize though he cannot yet perform them. So too in language acquisition: as in all forms of assisted learning, it depends massively upon participation in a dialogue, carefully stabilized by the adult partner.   (p. xiv)

For Bruner, cognitive development "depends upon a systematic and contingent interaction between a tutor and a learner," and teaching, therefore, is driven by language, "which ends by being not only the medium for exchange but the instrument that the learner[s] can then use [themselves] in bringing order into the environment" (Bruner 1966:6). The image of the teacher scaffolding learners so they can express what they would be unable to express on their own provides a helpful metaphor for appreciating the strategic role played by teacher questions and interactional feedback, which will be further explored in Chapter 4.

A socio-cognitive view contributes substantially to our understanding of the central role played by interaction in classroom learning, and is also complementary to a social-constructivist view of education, which entails presentation of "issues, concepts, and tasks in the form of problems to be explored in dialogue rather than as information to be ingested and reproduced" (Williams & Burden, 1997). According to this view, the essence of learning and teaching is found in student-teacher interaction where "the most valuable talk occurs in the context of exploration of events and ideas in which alternative accounts and explanations are considered and evaluated" (Wells 2001:3). Having gained considerable currency in the field of education and considered particularly relevant to science education, a social-constructivist view of learning as the co-construction of knowledge is predicated on the psychological and cultural relativity that underlies human perception and the variable nature of knowledge shaped by presupposition (e.g., Bruner 1971, 1986). Scientific knowledge, in this view, is seen "as tentative and as our best attempt to explain how and why things happen in the natural world" (Day & Shapson 1996:45). In immersion classrooms, Laplante (1997) argued for an approach in which science content is negotiated and language serves as a cognitive tool to enable learners to interact with scientific discourse in various modes. Learners need to actively participate in the co-construction of knowledge, "bringing prior beliefs to experiences and gradually modifying their beliefs as they interact with new experiences and the ideas of others" (Day & Shapson 1996:45). A constructivist approach applies well to history classes as well where students are encouraged to "construct a coherent narrative or expository historical account that carries both multiple perspectives and a sense of layering – of event as it occurred, event as it was recorded, and event as it was interpreted" (August & Hakuta 1997:66). With its emphasis on learning through interaction and its potential for minimizing transmission models of instruction, a social-constructivist approach has much to contribute to content-based instruction. There is considerable potential in instructional approaches that encourage students to use the target language not only as a communicative tool but also as a cognitive tool for interacting with the teacher, with one another, and with content knowledge itself.

5.   Purpose of this book

One of the most widely substantiated outcomes of immersion programs is that students' first language development and academic achievement are similar to (or better than) those of non-immersion students. Genesee (2004) confirmed that these findings "have been replicated, for the most part, in other regions of the world where similar programs with majority language students have been implemented" (p. 551; see also Christian & Genesee 2001; Johnson & Swain 1997). Another finding that is common across immersion programs is that students develop much higher levels of second language proficiency than do non-immersion students studying the second language as a subject for about 40 minutes each day. At the same time, research on the second language proficiency of French immersion students in Canada suggests that even higher levels of proficiency approximating native-speaker norms of grammatical and sociolinguistic competencies might be attainable through improved instructional strategies. Important to acknowledge, however, is that "functional bilingualism" – the oft-cited goal of immersion and content-based instruction – "is a vague and relative notion and can mean anything from the ability to understand and make oneself understood and get by in everyday social situations to the ability to function like a well-educated native-speaker in demanding social and professional settings" (Day & Shapson 1996:91). In this regard, Genesee (2004:549) provided a helpful definition of bilingual competence as "the ability to use the target languages effectively and appropriately for authentic personal, education, social, and/or work-related purposes." For students to reach this level of bilingual competence, however, instructional practices in immersion and content-based classrooms need to be rethought and refreshed. There is scope for improvement in immersion and content-based instructional approaches and, thus, much potential for refining pedagogical know-how and enhancing learning outcomes. This book aims to contribute to such a renewal.

This book is about effective instructional strategies that have been observed in classrooms and investigated empirically. This book is not about ideal program models or optimal starting points. As Genesee (2004) argued, "the notion that there is 'an optimal starting grade' for bilingual education is misguided since what might be 'optimal' in one community may not be in another" (p. 559). This book addresses the quality of instruction in immersion and content-based classrooms with a view to investing teachers with knowledge about findings from classroom-based research so they can reflect further on and experiment with a wider range of instructional options. Given their predominant focus on meaning, immersion and other content-based classrooms provide a rich context for reflecting on and experimenting with innovative ways of second language teaching and learning. Immersion and content-based classrooms replicate conditions for sustained exposure and authentic communication more than most other types of second language classrooms insofar as the target language is used purposefully to study other subjects, thus providing, theoretically at least, classroom settings with optimal conditions for language learning.

This book presents a synthesis of empirical research that has helped to shape evolving perspectives of content-based instruction since the introduction of immersion programs in Montreal more the 40 years ago. Drawing on classroom-based research, the book attempts to secure a more prominent place for the 'classroom' in classroom second language acquisition (SLA) research, bringing into play a socio-cognitive perspective to portray, on the one hand, how classroom learners process a second language through content and, on the other, how both teacher and students interact to negotiate language through content. In Chapter 2, a range of instructional practices observed in immersion and content-based classrooms is identified, to set the stage for justifying a counterbalanced approach that integrates both content-based and form-focused instructional options as complementary ways of intervening to develop a learner's interlanguage system. Incorporating both form-focused and content-based instruction, counterbalanced instruction brings together a wide range of opportunities for learners, on the one hand, to process language through content by means of comprehension, awareness, and production mechanisms (Chapter 3), and, on the other, to negotiate language through content by means of interactional strategies that involve teacher scaffolding and feedback (Chapter 4). Counterbalanced instruction is further expounded in the final chapter (Chapter 5) in an attempt to provide a fresh perspective on integrating language and content in ways that engage learners with language across the entire curriculum.

CHAPTER 2

Instructional practices at the interface of language and content

Claudette, a Grade 7 immersion teacher described by Day and Shapson (1996), created a language-rich science classroom that was a veritable arena of communication. Her students engaged in both 'doing' science and collaboratively talking about it. Students were encouraged to speculate, justify, and be comfortable with the view that there might be 'no right answer' to some questions, even though the teacher had clear learning objectives and structured her classes accordingly. Many opportunities for students to produce the second language and to communicate with one another arose inherently out of what was being learned, fusing language and science "into a unified whole" (p. 55) and enabling students to use a wide variety of language functions and structures. Similarly, Mme Legault, a Grade 1 immersion teacher described by Laplante (1993), counterbalanced language and content instruction as she interacted with students during science lessons. She provided rich and varied input and then helped students to improve the form and content of their own utterances by providing feedback that included questions, paraphrases, comments, translation, elaboration, and requests for translation or elaboration. Her interaction with students had a pedagogical function that encouraged language production on the part of the students and allowed them to negotiate the unfolding of certain activities.

Notwithstanding such excellent examples of teachers adept at integrating language with content, still other classroom observation studies suggest that the integration of language and content in content-based classrooms is far from a fait accompli. Swain (1996), for example, observed that "there is a lot of content teaching that occurs where little or no attention is paid to students' target language use; and there is a lot of language teaching that is done in the absence of context laden with meaning" (p. 530). Swain (1988) identified specific shortcomings, which, unless compensated for, restrict the effectiveness of content-based instruction. For example, she found that immersion teachers tended to provide learners with inconsistent feedback and that students were able to understand the content without necessarily engaging in some sort of form-function analysis. She also noted that content instruction did not invite much student production and was restricted in the range of language functions it generated.

In order to more effectively integrate language and content in content-based instruction, Stern (1990, 1992) argued that "analytic" and "experiential" instructional options need to be viewed as complementary, not as dichotomous (see also Allen, Swain, & Harley 1988; Allen et al. 1990). He characterized analytic strategies as those that emphasize accuracy and that focus on aspects of the linguistic code (including phonology, grammar, functions, discourse, and sociolinguistics), and which entail the study and practice of language items and rehearsal of second language skills. Experiential strategies entail non-language themes and topics as content, engage students in purposeful tasks, and emphasize the conveyance of meaning, fluency over accuracy, and authentic use of the target language. Stern (1992) recommended more systematic integration of analytic strategies in contexts of immersion and content-based instruction. At the same time, he recommended increased emphasis on experiential strategies in traditional programs where the target language is taught as a subject. In the spirit of instructional counterbalance, this book explores how the dichotomous view of analytic and experiential instructional options can be diffused to ensure a complementary integration of both. The aim of this particular chapter is to identify various instructional practices that have been observed in immersion and content-based classrooms with a view to identifying those that are most propitious for integrating language and content. Content-based instruction that only alludes to language incidentally falls short of full-fledged integration, and decontextualized grammar instruction, by definition, precludes integration. Form-focused instruction is most propitious for integrating language with content, especially as it draws on various literacy-based approaches underlying the school curriculum.

1.   Incidental focus on language

In their immersion classroom observation study, Swain and Carroll (1987) noted an important paradox: "Although one goal of immersion is to learn language through learning content, a general observation about the classes is that form and function are kept surprisingly distinct" (p. 191). They found that it was relatively rare for teachers (a) to refer during content-based lessons to what had been presented in a grammar lesson and (b) to set up content-based activities specifically to focus on form related to meaning. The observed tendency for teachers to avoid language issues during content-based instruction and instead to wait for language arts lessons to address language structure in relatively traditional ways may be the result of equivocal messages about the nature of language instruction in content-based approaches. 'Incidental' is a word that was initially attributed to the process of both teaching and learning language through content (e.g., Genesee 1987; Snow 1989; Swain & Lapkin 1982; more recently, see Long 2007), usually with a disclaimer, however, that 'incidental' is neither tantamount to 'haphazard' (Snow 1989) nor at odds with systematicity (Genesee 1987). Yet, it remains unclear how an incidental approach to language instruction can, at the same time, be systematic. Incidental learning is generally defined as learning without the intent to learn (or the learning of one thing when the learner's primary objective is to do something else; see Schmidt 1994). Incidental language instruction is encapsulated by Long's (1991) notion of "focus on form" in which teachers, while teaching content other than language itself (e.g., biology, mathematics, geography), "overtly draw students' attention to linguistic elements as they arise incidentally in lessons whose overriding focus is on meaning" (p. 46). This section aims to illustrate that much incidental attention to language is too brief and likely too perfunctory to convey sufficient information about certain grammatical subsystems and thus, in those cases, can be considered neither systematic nor apt to make the most of content-based instruction as a means for teaching language.

Based on interviews with elementary-level immersion teachers, Netten (1991) reported that their instructional strategies were not affected by the fact that they were teaching both content and a second language: "Teachers expected that the pupils would learn the target language as they were learning the content of the prescribed curriculum" (p. 288). Issues relating to second language development were not a prime concern for the immersion teachers observed by Salomone (1992a) either. Discipline was their top priority, followed by content learning, then second language development. One of the Grade 1 French immersion teachers, for example, perceived herself as a subject-matter teacher and not as a language teacher: "From nine until three-thirty, I do not teach French. I teach subject matter, and French is learned through this content" (Salomone 1992a: 22). Two of the teachers described by Lyster (1998d), also in elementary immersion classrooms, claimed to have only a vague idea of how they focused on language as they interacted with students because, they both acknowledged, "their real concern was content" (p. 74). Substantiating the findings of Allen et al. (1990) and Swain (1988), Day and Shapson (1996) found that attention to form/meaning relationships and use of corrective feedback were infrequent during science classes taught in the immersion language.

Even in the case of mainstream classrooms with two teachers – a subject-matter specialist working in partnership with a specialist of English as a second language (ESL) – institutional constraints appear to militate against equitable integration of content and language. In her study of ESL students in mainstream classrooms in the UK, for example, Creese (2002) observed that "knowledge about language was positioned as less important in the subject classroom. Knowledge and pedagogies associated with language learning and languages for learning were pushed to the periphery of the schools' agendas" (p. 611; see also Arkoudis 2006; Creese 2006). Short's (2002) observational study of four teachers in sheltered ESL middle school classrooms in the US included two teachers trained as ESL instructors and two with certification as social studies instructors. Her analysis of 14 hours of classroom interaction revealed that, of 3,044 teacher utterances, 44% addressed content, 35% addressed tasks, and only 20% addressed language. Even the trained ESL teachers devoted only one fifth or less of their interactions to language. Of the 623 teacher utterances that did address language, 95% focused on vocabulary comprehension or pronunciation. Short attributed these findings to the pressure that teachers in sheltered classrooms feel as they prepare students for state and local testing, and also to the content specialists' lack of background in language. In fact, one of the social studies teachers said about language teaching: "I thought that was someone else's job" (p. 21). Having observed many teachable moments for language teaching slip away, Short concluded that both ESL and content teachers alike need to expand their conception of language beyond vocabulary comprehension to include explicit instruction in language learning strategies, language functions, vocabulary, grammar, mechanics, and the four language skills.

One way for teachers to integrate language instruction more systematically into content-based instruction is to identify "content-obligatory language" (Snow et al. 1989), which students need to know in order to study subject matter through their second language. Content-obligatory language includes technical vocabulary and other domain-specific expressions. In addition, it includes language functions that predominate in a particular content area, such as informing, defining, analyzing, classifying, predicting, inferring, explaining, and justifying (Cloud et al. 2000). A good example of this type of language and content integration was illustrated by Early's (2001) study of language and content specialists collaborating in Grade 6 social studies lessons to teach about the Mesopotamians:

> The classroom teacher used the timeline to give the students an overview of how long the civilizations had lasted, their relative time in power, a few of their major achievements, and the impression that these civilizations were important and had made significant contributions. The ESL support teacher used the timeline to explicitly develop the concept of 'sequence' and the language used in sequence texts, for example, 'began in…' and 'ended in…'; 'the first community was…'; 'followed by…'; 'next came the …'; 'finally…'; 'the … lived from… to …'; and the past tense. Orally, the students produced a wide variety of possible linguistic realizations of the timeline.   (p. 170)

Because it otherwise lacks such an intentional and systematic focus on language, an incidental approach to teaching language through content, to borrow the encapsulating title of Swain's (1988) seminal paper, falls inadequately short of "manipulating and complementing content teaching to maximize second language learning." Content-based instruction that draws students' attention only incidentally to language provides substantial exposure to contextualized language use and promotes primarily lexically oriented learning, but does not ensure the learning of less salient yet crucial morphosyntactic features of the target language (Harley 1994; Swain 1988).

1.1 Linguistic challenges

Incidental attention drawn to language during subject-matter instruction is insufficient because, without having their attention drawn more systematically to the target language, the cognitive predispositions of second language learners interact with classroom input in ways that restrict the incidental assimilation of specific target features and grammatical subsystems, such as verbs, pronouns, and gender in the case of French immersion students. This section illustrates how content-based instruction, either on its own or in conjunction with incidental reference to language, falls short of facilitating entry into each of these important grammatical subsystems.

The attested shortcomings in French immersion students' second language proficiency cannot be easily compared to similar shortcomings that may or may not occur in other immersion languages, which range from Spanish, Catalan, Swedish, German, and English, to Basque, Estonian, Japanese, Mandarin, and several less commonly taught languages. Yet there exists at least one systematic proposal for identifying problematic features of any target language taught primarily through subject-matter instruction. Harley (1993) identified the following classes of target features as problem areas that require explicit attention in content-based classrooms:

-   features that differ in non-obvious or unexpected ways from the first language
-   features that are irregular, infrequent, or otherwise lacking in perceptual salience in the second language input
-   features that do not carry a heavy communicative load

In this view, the persistent difficulties experienced by French immersion students in their acquisition of various aspects of the verbal system, pronominal reference, and gender attribution result from an interaction among (a) the incongruence of these subsystems with students' first language, (b) their lack of prominence in the discourse of subject-matter instruction, and (c) their redundancy in communicative interaction. With respect to redundancy, for example, Ellis (1986) argued that "it is not efficient to operate a system in which two forms have total identity of function" and that "unless alternative forms can be justified by allocating them to different functions, redundant forms will be eliminated from the interlanguage" (p. 95). From the perspective of second language learners of French, therefore, imperfective verb forms might appear redundant relative to perfective verb forms, plural second-person pronouns might appear redundant relative to singular forms, and feminine determiners might appear redundant relative to masculine forms.

Readers unfamiliar with French are encouraged to identify, in another target language, features known to be difficult to learn through content instruction for reasons similar to those proposed in this chapter to explain why basic subsystems such as verbs, pronouns, and gender are so challenging. Features that have been identified as difficult for many second language learners of English, for example, include question formation (e.g., Lightbown & Spada 1990; Mackey 1999), articles (e.g., Muranoi 2000; Sheen, in press), relative pronouns (e.g., Doughty 1991), possessive determiners (e.g., Spada, Lightbown, & White 2005; White 1998), adverb placement (Trahey & White 1993), tense and aspect (e.g., Bardovi-Harlig 2000; Collins 2002), past tense forms (Doughty & Varela 1998; Ellis, Loewen, & Erlam 2006), and dative constructions (Carroll & Swain 1993; McDonough 2006). Important to appreciate is that some features require instruction more than others and, in fact, many target features do not necessarily require any instructional emphasis at all because they can be easily acquired through exposure to content-based instruction. For example, phonologically salient and high-frequency lexical items with syntactic patterns congruent with a learner's first language are known to be acquired with relative ease through rich exposure to content instruction (Harley 1994). That not all target features are equally easy or difficult to acquire results from a complex interaction of their structural properties and occurrence in classroom input with a learner's own developing system of linguistic representations and cognitive processing (Long 1996). To identify problem areas, some degree of interlanguage analysis is necessary, as was the case for the features outlined forthwith.

1.1.1 *Verb system*

Imagine a Grade 6 class of students listening to their teacher initiate the following discussion in their second language about 18th-century life in the Antilles:

> *How do you think these plantations ... are going ... to change ... life in the Antilles? [...] These people are going to sell their sugar, rum, molasses, brown sugar. They are going to make money. With the money, they are going to buy clothes, furniture, horses, carriages ... all they want and they are going to bring them back to the Antilles.*   (Swain 1996:533)

Even though this is a history lesson about events that took place more than 200 years ago, the teacher uses the immediate future tense to convey her message. Swain described the teacher's choice of tense as "superb from a content teaching point of view... Its use has brought the distant past into the lives of the children, got them involved, and undoubtedly helped them to understand the social and economic principle that this historical unit was intended to demonstrate. However, as a language lesson modeling past tense usage, it was less than a success" (Swain 1996:533). Because the verb system is a "centrally important area of the structure of a language which is likely to be a major hurdle for learners of any age" (Harley 1986:59), leaving it to chance, as opportunities arise (or not) during content-based instruction, is likely to have detrimental effects on second language development. Early immersion students are indeed known to have trouble with verbs even after several years in the program. In the context of immersion, research has documented difficulties that students experience in using the verb system to express aspectual distinctions, hypothetical modality, and directional motion.

One of most persistent problems for learners of French as a second language is the distinction between perfective and imperfective past tenses (*passé composé* and *imparfait*, respectively). The functional distinctions between these two tenses are especially challenging for anglophone learners of French, because the form/meaning mappings of these tenses are not clear-cut across French and English. As Spada et al. (2005) argued, target features in which there is a misleading similarity between the first and second language for expressing the same meaning are prime targets for explicit instruction, because such features are those that second language learners "are most likely to have long term difficulty acquiring through communicative interaction" (p. 201). Research has indeed shown that even advanced immersion students continue to use perfective and imperfective tenses in non-nativelike ways, overusing the *passé composé* with action verbs and underusing the *imparfait* to refer to habitual past actions (Harley 1992). In addition to the challenging effects of lexical aspect and first language influence on their acquisition of tense-aspect marking in their second language, immersion students are confronted with temporal distinctions that are difficult in some contexts for learners to notice in oral input. For example, whereas the written forms of *j'ai mangé* and *je mangeais* are clearly distinguishable, their oral forms in some spoken varieties of French are not.

With respect to modality, research has shown that immersion students' ability to understand the hypothetical meaning of conditionals far exceeds their ability to correctly produce conditionals (e.g., Harley & Swain 1984). The causes of students' shortcomings in production are at least three-fold. First, the conditional in French is derivative and dependent on verbal inflections that are morphologically more complex than the English conditional, which consists of the modal verb *would* followed by a simple verb stem. Second, learners can easily avoid the conditional and still express hypothetical meaning without causing much misunderstanding. For example, when the need arises to express the notion of uncertain possibility in the future, learners who are unable to produce conditionals can resort to simpler means of expression, by opting for the *futur simple* or even the *futur proche* in conjunction with invariable adverbs such as *probablement* and *peut-être* to add modal value (Harley 1992). A third factor is low frequency in classroom discourse.

With respect to the range of verb tenses in teacher-talk, Harley et al. (1987) reported the findings of more than 28 hours of observations of 19 French immersion teachers in the province of Ontario in the 1980s. They found that 75% of all verbs used were restricted to the present tense or imperative forms, whereas only 15% were in the past tense, 6% were in the future tense, and 3% were in the conditional mood. Table 1 compares these results with those of Izquierdo (in progress) who found in his analysis of six French immersion teachers observed for 28 hours in Montreal schools in the 1990s that the percentage distribution of verbs they used was identical to Harley et al.'s findings. This comparison confirms that the range of grammatical forms available in content-based input is limited, even over time and across geographic settings, and goes a long way in explaining gaps in students' second language development, especially their limited use of conditional forms and their inaccurate use of past tense forms.

Table 1. Percentage distribution of verb tenses used by immersion teachers

	Ontario	Québec
Present/imperative	75	74
Past	15	14
Future	6	8
Conditional	3	3
Other	1	1
Total	100%	100%

Note: Ontario: 28.5 hrs; 19 teachers; Grades 3/6
*   Québec: 28 hrs; 6 teachers; Grades 4–6*

Another challenging feature of verbs for immersion students concerns lexical choices and the syntactic frames of verbs that express motion and directionality, as documented by Harley (1992; Harley & King 1989). Whereas English verbs of motion tend to combine motion with manner, French verbs of motion combine motion with direction. Prepositions are thus commonly used in English to express directionality (e.g., He came *down* the stairs) while in French the notion of direction is contained in the verb (*Il a descendu l'escalier*). Influenced by English, French immersion students, in comparison to native speakers, use substantially fewer high-frequency directional motion verbs, such as *arriver, descendre, monter, partir, passer, redescendre, rentrer,* and *sortir*. The result is not necessarily erroneous syntax but does reveal clear differences from native norms. Immersion students show a clear preference for verbs whose syntactic frames are more similar to verbs in English, using most frequently the high-coverage verbs *aller* and *venir* but with prepositions that parallel English usage, resulting in phrases like '*Elle est allée dans la maison*' instead of the more native-like '*Elle est rentrée*' (Harley & King 1989). (Note that the avoidance of verbs of motion is not the same problem as that also identified by Harley 1993, whereby immersion students confound the auxiliary verbs *avoir* and *être*.)

1.1.2 *Second-person pronouns*
Personal pronouns are an essential part of any language. First- and second-person pronouns serve respectively to identify the speaker and listener(s) in any given speech situation, whereas third-person pronouns provide efficient and cohesive ways of referring to anyone or anything not involved as speaker or listener. In French, in addition to making these distinctions in person, most personal pronouns make distinctions in number, some make distinctions in gender, and others imply differences in status. At an early stage, from exposure alone, immersion students are able to sort out basic subject pronouns, learning

initially at least one subject pronoun for each person (Harley 1980). Third-person subject pronouns, however, present a learning problem, in both number and gender, while third-person object pronouns present an even greater challenge. With respect to second-person pronouns in French, the choice of appropriate forms – even though at first glance this finding might seem surprising – continues to be a significant source of confusion for students. The development of an accurate system of second-person reference is not a straightforward process for young anglophone learners of French in early immersion classrooms (Lyster & Rebuffot 2002; Swain & Lapkin 1990).

Lyster and Rebuffot's (2002) discourse analysis of classroom input showed that, in addition to serving as a second-person pronoun of address to mark singular and familiar reference, *tu* indicates indefinite reference and even plural reference in discourse contexts where a teacher's need to express intimacy or solidarity with young children competes with the need to express plurality. Although infrequent in the linguistic environment, a teacher's use of *tu* forms with seemingly plural referents seems to provide sufficient positive evidence to young learners that *tu* can serve as an all-encompassing second-person pronoun. In the absence of negative evidence, young learners are induced to over-generalize the functions of *tu* because it corresponds precisely with their cognitive predisposition for selectively attending to only one second-person pronoun that is equivalent to *you*. This kind of split, where a single form in the first language is manifest as two or more in the target language, is often considered a prime source of difficulty for language learners who, for the sake of economy, may adopt one form at the expense of the other (Ellis 1986). Moreover, interlanguage forms that develop as a result of both first language influence and ambiguous input are especially recalcitrant in homogeneous classrooms where learners share the same first language (Lightbown 1992). The result is "sociolectal variation" whereby the social connotations associated with *vous* are lost but the notional meaning underlying second-person pronominal reference is still evoked, "since the speaker is left with at least one variant to express whatever notional meaning the formal and informal variants convey" (Mougeon & Beniak 1991:223).

Swain and Carroll (1987) found that immersion teachers' use of singular *vous* as a politeness marker was almost completely absent from classroom discourse, whereas plural *vous* was indeed available in the input and used equally often as singular *tu*. The absence of singular *vous* in the teachers' input helps to explain its absence from immersion students' sociolinguistic repertoire (Swain & Lapkin 1990). Once more these descriptive findings of immersion teacher input in Ontario schools in the 1980s were substantiated by a follow-up study in

Table 2. Percentage distribution of *tu* and *vous* used by immersion teachers

	Ontario	Québec
Tu-singular	46.0	52.0
Tu-plural	3.7	2.4
Tu-generic	3.0	1.2
Vous-singular	0.9	0.3
Vous-plural	44.5	43.8
Vous-generic	1.9	0.3
Total	100%	100%

Note: Ontario: 15 hrs; 10 teachers; Grade 6
Québec: 6.5 hrs; 6 teachers; Grades 4–6

Montreal schools in the 1990s. Table 2 presents a comparison of Barret's (2000) findings in Montreal and those of Swain and Carroll (1987) in Ontario with respect to singular, plural, and generic uses of *tu* and *vous* by immersion teachers. The almost identical distributions across time and space suggest yet again functional constraints and also inflexibility in the use of classroom language, even when used for subject-matter instruction.

Moreover, attention drawn only incidentally to sociostylistic variation has proven insufficient for developing sociolinguistic competence and pragmatic awareness in classroom settings (see Kasper 2001; Schmidt 1993). Incidental teacher remarks specifically about second-person reference are not only insufficient to help students clarify and consolidate their already precarious knowledge of this important distinction, but may even be misleading. For example, a teacher observed by Salomone (1992a:34) remarked incidentally to her students: "*Que voyez-vous? Que vois-tu? On peut dire les deux.*" *Tu* and *vous*, however, are not interchangeable forms, being instead constrained by both grammatical and social contexts. In a classroom intervention study by Lyster (1994a) addressing these and other social markers, frequency of exposure to *vous* and to conditional forms was held constant, while students' attention was drawn intentionally to second-person pronouns but only incidentally to conditional forms. Results clearly showed that learners made huge gains in their ability to use *vous* appropriately, but no gains in their use of the conditional as a politeness marker.

1.1.3 *Grammatical gender*

A puzzling and extreme example of the difference between first and second language acquisition is evident in the seemingly effortless and flawless acquisition of grammatical gender by native speakers of French on the one hand, and the notoriously difficult and often incomplete acquisition of this same grammatical subsystem by many second language learners of French on the other. Karmiloff-Smith (1979:167) reported that, by the age of 3–4 years old, French-speaking children develop "a very powerful, implicit system" for accurate gender attribution. In contrast, Tucker, Lambert, and Rigault (1977:11) remarked that "the necessity to master grammatical gender may be the single most frustrating and difficult part of the study of French as a second language." Even after many years of classroom exposure to French, immersion students fall short of using grammatical gender with much accuracy (e.g., Harley 1979, 1998). Lyster (2006) reported that immersion students were about three times more likely to accurately assign masculine gender than to accurately assign feminine gender. Carroll (1989) observed that "English-speaking children in immersion programs have problems producing gender markers not only in spontaneous production but also in controlled experimental situations. They do not appear to have anything resembling native competence" (p. 575).

Grammatical gender markers are not salient in classroom discourse, in spite of their frequency; nor do they convey, in the case of inanimate nouns, any semantic distinctions. Moreover, grammatical gender does not exist in English. Carroll (1989) proposed that native speakers of French acquire and process determiners and nouns as co-indexed chunks, whereas anglophone learners of French acquire and process determiners and nouns as distinct syntactic words and independent phonological units. Influenced by the many French grammarians who claim that grammatical gender is arbitrary and unsystematic in the case of inanimate nouns (e.g., Bérard & Lavenne 1991; Bosquart 1998; Jacob & Laurin 1994), teachers encourage students to learn gender attribution on an item-by-item basis, and often do so through incidental reminders. Lyster (1993) observed a teacher who, after coming across too many gender errors in his students' written work, reminded students that "guessing gender is simply not good enough" and insisted they use dictionaries to verify. Swain and Carroll (1987:237–238) observed the following teacher-student exchange in which students assessed their fellow students' performance in a play:

> S1:   *J'ai pensé uhm qu'elle était très bonne parce que sa voix était très fort.*
> [I thought um she was really good because her voice-F was very loud-M.]
>
> T: *Sa voix était très forte. C'est vrai, oui.* [Her voice-F was very loud-F. That's true, yes.]

> S2:   *Je pense que c'était très bon parce qu'elle avait beaucoup d'expression dans son/son voix.* [I think that it was very good because she had a lot of expression in her/her voice-M.]
>
> S3:   *X était excellent /?/ uhm voix très fort et beaucoup d'expression.* [X was excellent because /?/ um voice very loud-M and a lot of expression.]
>
> T: *Oui, excellent, voix très forte, beaucoup d'expression.* [Yes, excellent, voice very loud-F, lots of expression.]
>
> S4:   *euh sa voix était très euh* [um her voice-F was very um]
>
> T: *Forte* [loud-F]
>
> S4:   *Fort mais je pense qu'il peut avoir un peu plus de uhm d'expression.* [Loud-M but I think there could be more um expression.]
>
> T: *Un peu plus d'expression, la voix très forte, oui.* [A bit more expression, very loud-F voice.]
>
> S5:   */?/ bon voix* [/?/ good-M voice]
>
> T: *Il a une très bonne voix, oui.* [He has a very good-F voice.]
>
> S6:   *Je pensais que son voix était* [I thought that his voice-M]
>
> T: *Sa* [His-F]
>
> S6:   *Sa voix était très bien mais /?/* [His voice-F was very good but /?/]

Swain and Carroll (1987:239) provided the following commentary, which highlights just how unsystematic (and inconsistent) such an incidental approach can be:

> Although the teacher provides students with feedback about the gender of *voix*, the message is a confusing one. In one case, no indication is given that the student is incorrect, even though the student is clearly hesitant: *son/son voix*. In several instances the teacher repeats the student, correcting the error as she does. However, in another instance, the teacher repeats the student, correcting one error but leaving another: *voix très forte*. If the message is that what the teacher repeats is correct, then the message is that *voix* does not need an article. In another instance the teacher provides the student with the correct adjective *forte*, which the student repeats as *fort*.

Similarly, when asked by students why the French word *planche* is feminine, a teacher observed by Salomone (1992b) responded, "There isn't any explanation. It's feminine and it's *une*. There's no trick. You just have to learn it like that" (pp. 101–102). Again, however, this incidental remark conveys misleading information, because there exists considerable evidence that gender attribution is largely rule-driven and based on word-internal structural properties. That is, contrary to assertions put forth in most French grammar books, Tucker et al.

(1977) found that grammatical gender entails a rule-governed subsystem, in which "distinctive characteristics of a noun's ending and its grammatical gender are systematically related" (p. 64). Similarly, in a recent analysis of nearly 10,000 nouns in *Le Robert Junior Illustré*, Lyster (2006) reported that 81% of all feminine nouns and 80% of all masculine nouns in the corpus proved to be rule governed, having endings whose orthographic representations systematically predict their gender. Gender attribution in French is a good example of a grammatical subsystem in need of a systematically derived pedagogical grammar to counter the unhelpful information available in traditional grammars. Moreover, gender attribution is a quintessential example of a grammatical subsystem that cannot be learned incidentally by second language learners through exposure to content-based instruction.

2.   Decontextualized grammar instruction

It is often reported that immersion and content-based approaches entail language learning through content alone, without any accompanying second language instruction. If ever there is attention drawn to language, this is reportedly done so incidentally. However, this is not an accurate representation. A great deal of language instruction has in fact been observed in immersion classrooms, although with indeterminate effectiveness. Incidental references to language (or none at all) have certainly been observed in subject-matter lessons, whereas language arts lessons tend towards a much more intentional and also explicit focus on language. Swain and Carroll (1987), for example, observed many lessons set aside to focus on grammar, during which time formal rules, paradigms, and grammatical categories were presented. These decontextualised grammar lessons emphasized the learning and categorizing of forms rather than relating these forms to their communicative functions, and appeared to have minimal effect on students whose exposure to the target language was primarily message-oriented and content-based (Swain 1996).

The fact that French immersion teachers have been observed teaching isolated grammar lessons may reflect their reality of having to rely on language arts material designed for native speakers. Lyster (1987) argued that such materials were inappropriate for second language learners, at least in the case of French with its well-known emphasis on structural analysis (Cazabon & Size-Cazabon 1987). He suggested that the continued use over the years of materials designed for native speakers could even contribute negatively to students' second language development by circumventing their specific language learning needs. He found that grammar materials designed for native speakers, but used in immersion classrooms, rarely required learners actually to choose forms in relation to their meaning and instead provided extensive practice in identifying parts of speech and parsing sentences in terms of structural components, as well as plenty of fill-in-the-blank practice in spelling homophonous verb forms. The latter derive from rules of grammatical spelling, which permeate language arts materials for native speakers, whose difficulties with homophony are notorious for persisting well into adulthood. Yet, students who are struggling with principles underlying basic grammatical subsystems arguably need more opportunities to sort out form/meaning mappings and fundamental distinctions known to be difficult for second language learners than opportunities for distinguishing homophonous spellings and for parsing sentences.

To gain further insight into the nature of language instruction during language arts lessons in immersion as well as mainstream classrooms, Fazio and Lyster (1998) compared French immersion classrooms, situated in English-language schools composed of a majority of anglophone students, with mainstream classrooms in French-language schools, intended for native speakers of French but comprising a large number of minority-language students. Through use of the Communicative Orientation to Language Teaching (COLT) observation scheme (Spada & Fröhlich 1995), profiles of two distinct learning environments emerged. The immersion context proved to be varied in its integration of analytic and experiential instructional options in language arts classes (see also Allen et al. 1990; Dicks 1992), including variety in classroom organization, content that focused on both language and other topics, and text that included extended and also authentic discourse (e.g., anthologies of short stories and legends, student-made reports, classified ads, recipes). In contrast, the language arts classes with mainstreamed minority-language students were almost exclusively analytic in their approach to language teaching. The content focus was primarily on language form and most materials entailed only minimal discourse (e.g., grammar textbooks, grammar workbooks, word lists), reflecting the activities observed in these classrooms, which included dictations and analyses of parts of speech, verb inflections, homonyms, sentence structure, and agreement rules. The prevalence of a predominantly analytic orientation in Grade 5 language arts classrooms composed of both native speakers and second language learners of French was an unexpected finding, given the trend in many North American classrooms for language arts instruction to include some aspects of whole language instruction. Fazio and Lyster concluded that learners in the minority-language setting would benefit from more experientially oriented intervention, based on Cummins' (1989) argument that minority-language students will benefit from and, moreover, be empowered by instructional interventions with an interactive/experiential orientation, whereas classrooms characterized by transmission models of pedagogy tend to disable such students.

The distinction between the "empowering" versus "disabling" effects of different instructional orientations was illustrated by Fazio and Lyster's (1998) comparison of isolated grammar lessons about homophones. In the mainstream classroom comprising both native speakers and second language learners of French, the children listened attentively as the teacher slowly read aloud an entire page of their grammar book about distinctions between *n'y* and *ni*. Then, one-by-one traveling across rows, the children took turns reading a sentence, adding the correct answer by saying then spelling the required homonym. As each correct answer was confirmed by the teacher, students wrote the answer in the blank on their page. In contrast, students in the French immersion class participated a great deal as they tested their hypotheses about the homophonous distinctions between *peu*, *peut*, and *peux*. Rather than asking students to fill in the blanks, the teacher pushed students to propose their own examples to show their understanding of the distinctions. In the French immersion class, therefore, discussion about language, some creativity, and even some student-initiated discourse, tended to replace the teacher-led drill observed in the class combining mainstreamed minority-language students with native speakers of French.

The lesson observed in the immersion classroom revealed that even a de-contextualized lesson about homonyms can be conducted in ways that generate enthusiasm and creativity. However, within immersion and content-based settings, teachers are well positioned to spend more time drawing attention to language in context during content-based instruction, and less time on de-contextualized grammar during language arts. Overemphasizing decontextualized language lessons at the expense of systematically drawing attention to language in the context of subject-matter instruction falls short of tapping the full potential of content-based classrooms. A clear example of exploiting this potential comes from a Grade 4 immersion classroom observed by Lyster (1998c). During a highly interactive lesson about meteorology, a student pointed out that there are two ways of saying 'meteorologist' in French: *météorologiste* or *météorologue*. The teacher immediately asked for the gender of these words, and the students agreed that both *météorologiste* and *météoro-logue* could be either masculine or feminine with no inflectional changes. She then asked students if they knew of other names of occupations whose forms do not change according to gender. As a result of lively and collective brainstorming, students came up with the following animate nouns: *vétéri-naire, dentiste, secrétaire, concièrge, élève, thérapeute, linguiste*. During their search for these words, the students experimented with several phonological distinctions (e.g., *directeur-directrice; poète-poétesse; illustrateur-illustratrice; instituteur-institutrice; assistant-assistante*) as well as purely orthographic distinctions (e.g., *professeur/e, auteur/e*).

These Grade 4 students thus demonstrated considerable knowledge of grammatical gender during this digression from their lesson about meteorologists. Yet, later that same morning, the teacher again focused on grammatical gender but did so in a decontextualized lesson, which was characterized by a narrow focus on metalanguage and formal categories. The teacher intended to draw students' attention to distinctions in grammatical gender, but her use of the term 'gender' (*genre* in French) outside of any meaningful context proved to be rather abstract and thus led to considerable confusion on the part of the students and frustration on the part of the teacher.

T: *Non. J'ai demandé le genre. Que c'est loin, le genre. Quel est le genre?*	T: *No. I asked for the gender. Gender's really far away! What's the gender?*
S1: *Le genre [?]*	S1: *Gender [?]*
T: *Non. Quel est le genre? Le genre, c'est quoi? D'abord on va commencer par le nombre. Le nombre, c'est quoi?*	T: *No. What's the gender? Gender, what is gender, anyway? First, we're going to begin with number. Number, what is that?*
S2: *Le nombre, c'est...*	S2: *Number is...*
T: *Combien qu'on a de nombres en français? [...]*	T: *Grammatical number refers to how many in French? [...]*
S3: *Neuf cents?*	S3: *Nine hundred?*
T: *Non. Le genre et le nombre, vous ne souvenez plus de ça?*	T: *No. Gender and number, you don't remember that?*
Ss: *Non.*	Ss: *No.*
T: *Aye-aye-aye. Il y a deux genres et il y a deux nombres. Le nombre, qu'est-ce que ça vous dit déjà? Oui?*	T: *Aye-aye-aye. There are two genders and two numbers. Number, what does that mean to you? Yes?*
S4: *Le genre, je sais. C'est, c'est [?]*	S4: *Gender, I know. It's, it's [?]*
T: *[...] De quel genre es-tu?*	T: *[...] What gender are you?*
S5: *Masculin?*	S5: *Masculine?*

T:	*Toi, tu es du genre masculin. Est-ce que c'est vrai?*		T:	*You are of masculine gender. Is that true?*
Ss:	*Non. Oui.*		Ss:	*No. Yes.*
T:	*Oui, bien sûr. Toi, de quel genre es-tu?*		R:	*Yes, of course. And what gender are you?*
S6:	*Féminin.*		S6:	*Feminine.*
T:	*Bon! … Bon, le nombre en français. c'est quoi le nombre, Stéphanie? Le nombre? Le genre, c'est féminin ou masculin. Le nombre, c'est quoi en français? C'est quoi le nombre?*		T:	*Good! … Now, number in French. What's number, Stéphanie? Number? Gender is feminine or masculine. Number, what is it in French? What's number?*
S7:	*C'est comme féminin et masculin?*		S7:	*It's like feminine and masculine?*
T:	*C'est comme féminin et masculin? Non, ça c'est le genre. Le nombre, c'est …*		T:	*It's like feminine and masculine? No, that's gender. Number is…*
S7:	*Singulier ou pluriel?*		S7:	*Singular or plural?*

The decontexualized nature of the lesson obfuscates grammatical gender, as students are asked to consider gender and number as naturally associated categories, owing arguably to their frequent juxtaposition in traditional grammars for the purpose of conveniently explaining agreement rules. Yet, gender and number are grammatical categories with purely formal links but no meaningful semantic association. Moreover, the teacher confounds grammatical and biological gender as she asks a boy and a girl to state their gender, as if this would help to clarify grammatical gender. Given the richness of meaningful contexts provided by subject matter in immersion and content-based classrooms, as evidenced by the spontaneous sequence of brainstorming earlier that day, one may well wonder about the need and utility of a decontexualized grammar lesson that confronts learners of this age with abstract metalanguage void of any meaningful context.

Lightbown (1998) argued that isolated grammar lessons may have only minimal effects in communicative or content-based classrooms because learners exposed to *language instruction* separately from meaningful *language use* are more likely to learn to treat language instruction as separate from language use. They will thus have difficulty transferring what they learn from language instruction to language use. In other words, language features learned in isolated grammar lessons may be remembered in similar contexts (e.g., during a grammar test), but hard to retrieve in the context of communicative interaction. Conversely, language features noticed in communicative interaction may be more easily retrieved in communicative contexts. Segalowitz (2000) explained this phenomenon in terms of *transfer-appropriate learning*, which posits that "a learning condition will be transfer appropriate if it activates cognitive operations that are likely to be reinstated later when the individual attempts to put the learning into practice" (p. 213). In other words, the kind of cognitive processing that occurs while performing learning tasks should ideally resemble the kind of processing involved during communicative language use. This provides a rationale for moving away from decontextualized grammar instruction and toward the integration of form-focused instruction.

3. Form-focused instruction

Immersion education exemplifies instructional settings where focus on meaningful content leads to the development of overall communicative ability, but with linguistic gaps in terms of accuracy. A great deal of research into the effects of form-focused instruction, therefore, has been undertaken in the context of immersion classrooms (for reviews see Lyster 1998c, 2004b; Swain 2000). Form-focused instruction refers to "any pedagogical effort which is used to draw the learners' attention to language form either implicitly or explicitly. This can include the direct teaching of language (e.g., through grammatical rules) and/or reactions to learners' errors (e.g., corrective feedback)" (Spada 1997:73). According to Ellis (2001), current research conceptualizes form-focused instruction "as a set of psycholinguistically motivated pedagogic options" (p. 12). Form-focused instructional options are generally considered most effective when implemented in communicative contexts, to ensure that learners will be able to transfer what they learn in the classroom to communicative interaction outside the classroom. Nonetheless, the extent to which form-focused instruction must be integrated into communicative activities is still open to debate (e.g., Ellis 2002; Lightbown 1998). Also open to further inquiry are the differential effects of form-focused instructional options that vary in degrees of explicitness, as well as the types of language features that can most benefit from form-focused instruction (see Doughty & Williams 1998; Ellis 2001; Lightbown & Spada 2006; Long & Robinson 1998; Norris & Ortega 2000; Spada 1997). Form-focused instruction has been portrayed as either "proactive" or "reactive" (Doughty & Williams 1998; Lyster 1998c; Lyster & Rebuffot

1996), but for optimal effectiveness both proactive and reactive approaches can be implemented in complementary fashion (Lyster 2004a, 2004b).

3.1 Proactive approaches

To attain the objectives of a truly integrated or holistic approach to second language development, Cloud et al. (2000) argued that the use of only one language textbook or series is insufficient. They recommended that immersion and content-based teachers should consider a textbook as only one of many resources, supplementing it appropriately, in order to provide language instruction that meets the needs of second language learners in content-based classrooms. The work required of teachers thus increases exponentially as they expand their use of resources beyond commercially available textbooks, developing instead alternative resources and creative ways of counterbalancing language and content throughout the curriculum. A solution that is proving more and more effective, but by no means reduces the amount of creativity and pedagogical know-how expected of teachers, is proactive form-focused instruction. Proactive form-focused instruction involves pre-planned instruction designed to enable students to notice and to use target language features that might otherwise not be used or even noticed in classroom discourse.

The effects of proactive form-focused instruction have been assessed in a set of classroom intervention studies targeting some of the grammatical subsystems identified previously as sources of ongoing difficulty (i.e., verbs, pronouns, gender). The studies were conducted by Harley (1989, 1998), Day and Shapson (1991), Lyster (1994a, 2004a), and Wright (1996) across various grade levels (2, 4, 5, 6, 7, 8) in urban schools in or near the cities of Vancouver, Toronto, and Montreal. The six studies spanned a period of 15 years, from 1989 to 2004, and involved over 1,200 students in 52 French immersion classrooms. Each study involved an intervention with a quasi-experimental design, enabling comparisons of at least two different groups of students: an experimental group exposed to a special form-focused instructional treatment and a comparison group exposed to only its regular immersion program. Pre-tests were given to all students in both experimental and comparison groups just prior to the pedagogical treatments, and then the form-focused instruction was administered only to students in the experimental groups for roughly 10 to 12 hours distributed over an average of 5 to 6 weeks. At the end of the instructional period, immediate post-tests were administered to all students. Then, several weeks later, delayed post-tests were administered to all students to assess the

Table 3. Quasi-experimental studies of form-focused instruction in French immersion classrooms

	Design features				Significant improvement (relative to Comparison group without instruction)	
	age of learners	target features	length of treatment	measures	immediate	delayed
Harley (1989)	11–12 (Grade 6)	*passé composé* & *imparfait*	12 hrs/ 8 weeks	Written production	no	no
				Cloze test	yes	no
				Oral production	yes	no
Day/Shapson (1991)	12–13 (Grade 7)	conditional mood	17 hrs/ 6 weeks	Written production	yes	yes
				Cloze test	yes	yes
				Oral production	no	no
Lyster (1994a)	13–14 (Grade 8)	second-person pronouns	12 hrs/ 5 weeks	Written production	yes	yes
				Multiple-choice test	yes	yes
				Oral production	yes	yes
Wright (1996)	9–11 (Grades 4/5)	verbs of motion	15 hrs/ 3 weeks	Written production	yes	yes
				Oral production	yes	yes
Harley (1998)	7–8 (Grade 2)	grammatical gender	8 hrs/ 5 weeks	Binary-choice test	yes	yes
				Aural discrimination	yes	yes
				Object identification	no	no
				Picture description	yes	yes
Lyster (2004a)	10–11 (Grade 5)	grammatical gender	9 hrs/ 5 weeks	Binary-choice test	recast & prompt groups	all treatment groups
				Text completion	all treatment groups	prompt group
				Object identification	prompt group	all treatment groups
				Picture description	prompt group	all treatment groups

extent to which they maintained over time what they had learned. A summary of the design and outcomes of these studies appears in Table 3.

Harley (1989) conducted a study in Grade 6 to determine the effects of form-focused instruction on students' use of perfective and imperfective past tenses in French. Students were assessed on three measures: a cloze test, a written production task, and an oral production task. Immediate post-test results revealed benefits on the cloze test and the oral task for the experimental group, but no significant differences on the written production task. No significant differences were found between the groups on any of the measures on a delayed post-test three months later. Day and Shapson (1991) conducted an intervention study with students in Grade 7 to test the effects of form-focused instruction on the use of the conditional mood in French. On immediate post-test measures, the experimental group demonstrated significant gains on a cloze test and a written composition, but not in oral production. Students maintained the significant gains on the composition and cloze test at the time of delayed post-testing 11 weeks later, but again showed no gains in oral production. Wright (1996) conducted a classroom intervention study with her Grade 4/5 immersion students to assess the effects of instruction on their use of verbs of motion in French (*amener, attraper, descendre, s'enfuir, entrer, filer, grimper, monter, passer, poursuivre, sortir, traverser*). Students exposed to the form-focused instruction improved significantly in their use of the target verbs in both oral and written production, relative to comparison classes, in both the short- and long-term. Lyster (1994a) examined the effect of form-focused instruction on the sociolinguistic competence of immersion students in Grade 8, focusing specifically on their use of second-person pronouns in formal and informal contexts. Test results showed significant improvement, both in the short- and long-term, in students' ability to accurately use second-person pronouns in formal contexts in both written and oral production tasks. Their overall awareness of sociolinguistic appropriateness, as demonstrated by their performance on multiple-choice tests, also improved significantly over time.

The prospect of providing young second language learners of French with opportunities to induce rules to help them predict the grammatical gender of large groups of nouns with similar endings motivated two quasi-experimental studies. Harley's (1998) study conducted with children in Grade 2 revealed significant long-term progress for students exposed to form-focused instruction, as demonstrated by three of the four measures (two listening tasks and an oral picture description task). The only measure that did not reveal significant improvement was an oral task requiring students to identify the gender of low-frequency unfamiliar nouns. Also focusing on grammatical gender, Lyster (2004a) conducted a classroom study with students in Grade 5. The treatment groups demonstrated significant long-term improvement at the time of delayed post-testing on both written measures and one of two oral measures; they had nonetheless shown short-term improvement on the other oral measure at the time of immediate post-testing.

The proactive form-focused instruction in these studies drew on elements from cognitive theory to emphasize (a) noticing and language awareness activities to enable learners to restructure interlanguage representations and (b) practice activities to enable learners to proceduralize more target-like representations. These studies will be referred to throughout the next chapter to illustrate instructional interventions designed to promote noticing and awareness as well as opportunities for practice. Then, in the final chapter, the need for instructional counterbalance will be invoked to explain the variable effectiveness of these instructional interventions.

3.2 Reactive approaches

Day and Shapson (1996) concluded from their case studies of immersion teachers that planned language teaching and "the many unplanned opportunities teachers can seize on to enhance language learning" (p. 81) are of equal importance. Corrective feedback as well as other attempts to draw learners' attention to language features in relatively unplanned and spontaneous ways are referred to as reactive form-focused approaches, because they occur in response to students' language production during teacher-student interaction. Research in support of reactive form-focused instruction suggests that it may be precisely at the moment when students have something to say that a focus on language can be most effective, rather than postponing a focus on language until a subsequent language arts lesson (Lightbown 1991, 1998; Lightbown & Spada 1990; Long 1991; Lyster 1998c, 1998d). Spada and Lightbown (1993:218) described one ESL teacher in particular who organized her teaching "in such a way as to draw the learners' attention to errors in their interlanguage development within the context of meaningful and sustained communicative interaction." Similarly, Lyster (1998d) described immersion teachers who, during content-based lessons, "were able to bring language form back into focus, without breaking the communicative flow, as they briefly negotiated form with students and then continued to interact with them about content" (p. 70). By drawing attention to language in this way, with the intention of helping students "to say what they themselves had already decided to say" (Lightbown 1991:211), teachers make use of ideal conditions for providing helpful feedback in a meaningful context. Despite the many obstacles arising at the interface of language and content teaching, examples abound in the research literature of teachers using reactive strategies to engage students with language during subject-matter instruction. Examples from Lapkin and Swain (1996) and Lyster (1998c) are presented here to illustrate that a reactive approach is ideal for pushing students in their lexical choices.

Lapkin and Swain (1996) described a Grade 8 immersion teacher, Leonard, who presented, in the form of a class "discussion," a combined science and language arts lesson on the greenhouse effect. In addition to focusing on meaning, Leonard drew attention to phonological, grammatical, sociolinguistic, and discourse-related aspects of vocabulary by using repetition and multiple synonyms, and also by revisiting words in different parts of the lesson. The extract below illustrates how he enhances the input to which students are exposed, first by introducing the synonyms *le rôle* and *la fonction*, and then the synonymous attributes *nocif, dangereux,* and *nuisible*:

1) T: *C'est un problème qui est*
        causé par les rayons du soleil.
        Et ce problème est provoqué
        aussi par la pollution, et il
        s'agit d'une certaine couche.
        [...] Quelle est la fonction,
        quel est le rôle de cette couche
        dans l'atmosphère?

1) T: *It's a problem caused by the*
        sun's rays. And this problem
        is also caused (provoked) by
        pollution, and there is a
        certain layer. [...] What is
        the function, what is the role
        of this layer in the
        atmosphere?

2) S: *Ça protégeait la terre des*
        rayons de soleil.

2) S: *It protected the earth from*
        the sun's rays.

3) T: *Elle nous protège contre les*
        rayons de soleil. Est-ce que
        tous les rayons de soleil sont
        nocifs? Qu'est-ce que ça veut
        dire 'nocif'?

3) T: *It protects us against the sun's*
        rays. Are all the sun's rays
        harmful? What does 'nocif'
        mean?

4) S1: *Dangereux.*

4) S1: *Dangerous.*

5) S2: *Qui nous cause, qui cause*
        du...

5) S2: *That causes us, that causes...*

6) S3: *Danger.*

6) S3: *Danger.*

7) T: *Oui, dangereux, nuisible,*
        nuisible à la santé.

7) T: *Yes, dangerous, harmful,*
        harmful to our health.

Swain (1996) commented, "In providing synonyms. Leonard is not simplifying his input; in fact these synonyms are a form of enrichment. ... This approach appears to have a direct impact on students' language development, as they use sophisticated vocabulary items in their initiations and responses in the lesson" (pp. 539–540).

Lyster (1998c) described a Grade 4 immersion teacher, Rachelle, who drew attention to relevant language features as she interacted with students during science and language arts lessons. During these lively discussions, she maintained a central focus on meaning yet succeeded in eliciting synonyms, antonyms, homophones, more precise terms, words with similar structural properties, as well as correct grammatical gender, spelling, and pronunciation. In the extract below, students are responding to her question about what a meteorologist does, while she seizes the opportunity to push them to refine their vocabulary:

1) S: *Ça dit qu'est-ce qui va*
        faire...

1) S: *It says what it's going to be*
        like...

2) T: *Ça dit? Qui ça dit?*

2) T: *It says? Who's 'it'?*

3) S: Ça explique...

4) T: Qui, ça? Dis-moi c'est qui, ça?

5) S1:   C'est les personnes qui...

6) T: Ah! C'est une personne! C'est une personne ici.

7) S2:   Une personne qui... qui dit... s'il va pleuvoir, s'il va faire du soleil, si...

8) S3:   C'est le /weatherman/

9) T: Qui dit...?

10) S4:   Qui dit la météo.

11) T: Qui dit la météo?

12) S5:   Qui annonce la température.

13) T: Qui annonce! Qui annonce la température. Est-ce qu'il ne fait qu'annoncer la température qu'on va avoir aujourd'hui...?

14) Ss: Non.

15) T: Qu'est-ce qu'il annonce aussi?

16) S5:   Demain.

17) T: Demain. Donc, il, aussi, il... demain il...?

18) S6:   Il prévient. [...]

19) T: Il nous prévient. Il prévoit.

20) S6:   Il prévient qu'il y aura des...

21) T: Il nous prévient. Il prévoit à l'avance, lui. Il prévoit à l'avance.

---

3) S: It explains...

4) T: Who's 'it'? Tell me who 'it' is.

5) S1:   It's persons...

6) T: Ah! It's a person! It's a person here.

7) S2:   A person who... who says... if it's going to rain or be sunny, if...

8) S3:   It's the /weatherman/ [in English].

9) T: Who says...?

10) S4:   Who says the weather.

11) T: Who says the weather?

12) S5:   Who announces the weather.

13) T: Who announces! Who announces the weather. Does he only announce the weather that we're going to have today...?

14) Ss: No.

15) T: What else does he announce?

16) S5:   Tomorrow.

17) T: Tomorrow. So, he, also, he... tomorrow he...?

18) S6:   He warns [...]

19) T: He warns us. He forecasts.

20) S6:   He warns that there will be...

21) T: He warns us. He forecasts in advance. He forecasts in advance.

As they propose what a meteorologist does, the students are led along a continuum from hearing and using general all-purpose verbs to more specific ones: *dire* ⇒ *expliquer* ⇒ *annoncer* ⇒ *prévenir* ⇒ *prévoir* (say ⇒ explain ⇒ announce ⇒ warn ⇒ forecast). In addition, Lyster (1994b) described a Grade

8 immersion teacher, Serge, whose reactive approach fostered "an interplay between communication and reflection on that communication through discussions on language use and group activities with an analytic focus" (Lyster 1994a: 279). Serge negotiated form as he interacted with his students during language arts lessons about sociostylistic variation, providing feedback to push students to be more precise and appropriate in their lexical choices and by asking questions that encouraged students to further develop or share their knowledge about language variation. Reactive approaches to form-focused instruction will be developed further in Chapter 4, which explores classroom interaction and the importance of scaffolding and feedback techniques.

4. Literacy instruction

Immersion and content-based classrooms provide rich contexts for seamlessly integrating form-focused instruction into literacy practices that fit within broader educational objectives. This is because at the core of early literacy instruction is the need to nurture learners' awareness of oral language and their ability to conceptualize language: "becoming aware of it as a separate structure, freeing it from its embeddedness in events" (Donaldson 1978: 90). Chapter 5 of Cloud et al.'s (2000) *Handbook for Enriched Education* provides a rich source of relevant information about teaching literacy in two languages, including a range of stage-appropriate instructional strategies to respond to learners' needs as they progress through predictable stages of literacy development, from pre-literacy to early/emergent literacy to late/intermediate literacy. According to Cloud et al. (2000), literacy instruction entails a holistic approach that (a) builds solidly on students' oral language and ensures its continued development, (b) teaches both text processing and production strategies, (c) develops decoding and encoding skills, and (d) creates a print-rich environment.

4.1 Sequencing instruction in two languages

The most popular approach to literacy instruction in Canadian early immersion programs introduces formal reading instruction in the second language in Grade 1 and delays first language instruction until Grades 2, 3, or 4. Results of this approach have consistently shown that early immersion students, as would be expected, experience a temporary lag in first language literacy skills, but only up to a year after language arts instruction in the first language has been introduced (Genesee 1987; Turnbull et al. 2001). The Canadian Association of Immersion Teachers (CAIT 1995) identified three other possible but less widely used approaches: (a) formal reading instruction in the first language and informal second language instruction in Grade 1, followed by formal reading instruction in the second language introduced in Grade 2; (b) concurrent literacy instruction in both languages; (c) formal reading instruction first in the second language along with informal attention to oral and listening skills in the first language. CAIT stressed that early development of second language literacy skills motivates young learners to communicate in the second language, and pointed out that a large body of research confirms that these students suffer no harm to their first language skills. For majority-language children such as those in immersion, Cloud et al. (2000) recommended that the second language "be used as the initial language of general academic instruction and the language in which reading and writing are first developed" (p. 88). They do not recommend concurrent initial literacy instruction in both languages, preferring "a sequential plan for formal reading/writing instruction so that teachers can ensure that their students have a firm foundation in reading/writing one language before beginning formal reading/writing instruction in the other" (p. 90). In her comparative study of English-speaking children in early and partial French immersion programs, Riches (2001) found that children who had learned first to read in the second language developed better second language reading skills than children who had learned to read simultaneously in both languages, and that, in both populations, first language reading skills were similar.

4.2 Whole language and process writing

Often implemented in conjunction with early literacy instruction, the 'whole language' approach to language development aims to ensure extensive exposure to the target language. Whole language in its purest form also minimizes explicit language instruction (including phonics instruction) and aims instead to integrate language skills across disciplines. With its emphasis on learning both oral and written language in the context of authentic use so that literacy tasks have a natural function, a whole language approach provides learners with meaningful opportunities to speak, write, and read in a range of personal and social contexts that include access to a variety of appropriate books and experience with literature. According to Hickman (1992), "with such strong ties to oral language learning, it seems that whole language should be a natural approach for immersion schooling" (p. 86).

Implementation of a whole language approach in content-based class-rooms, however, is not without particular challenges and criticisms. Hickman (1992) found that it was difficult for teachers to maintain the basic tenants of whole language in Grade 1 immersion classrooms: "Whole language teaching … assumes the possibility of encouraging social interaction and the empow-erment of students to use language to their own ends. These are difficult goals to achieve while children are watching the teacher for basic communication clues" (p. 94). Children in classrooms where whole language is implemented in their mother tongue are exposed to familiar and meaningful language not only at school but also at home and in the community. Children in immer-sion classrooms, Hickman found, turn their attention to the teacher for fa-miliar and meaningful exposure to the second language. Inevitably, there is also a lack of authentic texts and books in the second language that corre-spond appropriately and concurrently to students' linguistic ability, their age, and immediate interests. Moreover, as a constructivist activity, whole language encourages children's risk-taking and trial-and-error approaches to produc-ing language. Consequently, teachers accept forms derived from grammatical overgeneralizations, invented spellings, and meaningful approximations:

> Teachers are confident that children will develop facility with conventional forms by means of the feedback they get through experience with multiple sources of oral and written language. … When the teacher is the only pro-ficient language user within the child's world – school, home, community – it is only the teacher's response that can really help the child become more proficient. As the students themselves gain experience with print and as their classmates acquire the language and begin to respond to each other, this situ-ation becomes less critical. Still, however, the teacher is nudged toward a role that seems, by whole language standards, to be invested with undue authority. Nor is it a small matter that this role is exhausting; the teacher must talk, use gestures, act out, repeat, respond, write, read it back, and more.
>
> (Hickman 1992:95)

Hickman does not conclude, however, that a whole language approach is in-appropriate for content-based classrooms. Instead, she suggested that the ap-proach needs to be adapted when the target language is neither the mother tongue nor a language of the home or community and "the natural context for learning a language narrows to the school and classroom" (p. 96).

Genesee (1994b) also questioned some of the tenants of whole language, especially those that exclude any role for phonics in the teaching of reading and writing. Referring to extensive research conducted on children learning to read in their first language, he reiterated that phonemic awareness is the single most significant long-term predictor of success in learning to read. Cameron (2001) likened the well-known move away from phonics – and back again – to current interests in form-focused instruction:

> In the 80s, many teachers dropped phonics teaching in favour of whole language approaches that stressed overall meaning. In the 90s, it was found that many children were not succeeding in reading, and the blame was put on lack of phonics teaching. Now phonics is back, but combined with top-down and meaning-focused approaches to text. The parallels with the move to form-focus in communicative language teaching are striking. (Cameron 2001:133)

Whole language, however, as Genesee pointed out, means many things to different people. One definition described it as "an amorphous cluster of ideas about language development in the classroom" (Baker 2000:216), making it easy to adopt some of its tenants but not others. Cummins (2000), for example, advocated whole language as an appropriate approach, arguing that the basic notion of immersing children in literacy "is not at all incompatible with an explicit focus on teaching learning strategies and developing students' awareness of language, ranging from phonemic awareness in the early grades to the intersections of power and language in the later grades" (p. 259).

Another literacy-based approach in need of some tailoring for second language learners is the process approach to writing. Based on the premise that one learns to write by writing, process writing is an instructional approach that views writing as a set of dynamically interrelated stages characterized by negotiation with peers and teachers alike. The prewriting stage involves planning and collective brainstorming so that, ideally, students write about something they have already discussed orally. The writing stage entails drafting, revising, and editing. An important premise of process writing is that feedback is more useful on drafts than on the final product submitted for evaluation. In this regard, during the editing stage, Hall (1994) recommended the use of mini-lessons to address specific language issues, suggesting that immersion students receive personalized cards which they place in their writing folder in order to be reminded of errors to avoid. Early (2001) observed teachers effectively providing feedback about students' written work "in the context of collaborative conversations on the use of textual devices to construct meaning and position readers" (p. 169). Allen et al. (1990) stressed the importance of "systematically encouraging students to reflect on what they want to say and then helping them to make an appropriate choice of language forms" (p. 77). The final publishing stage of process writing is critical; Hall (1994) stressed that a variety of authentic audiences need to be sought (see also Allen et al. 1990) and that collaboration across grade levels provides valuable language practice. Within the school, for example, students can share their work with either younger or older students at other grade levels.

4.3 Vocabulary and reading instruction

With regard to reading instruction in later grade levels, Allen et al. (1990) observed an overemphasis on decoding difficult words during reading activities: "Students learned to pronounce words that they read aloud and to interpret passages, and the meanings of unfamiliar words were explained" (p. 64; see also Pica 2002). Allen et al. (1990) found that planned vocabulary instruction occupied "a rather narrow place" in the teachers' overall instructional approach: Teachers emphasized words associated with written language but not with speech; nor did they focus on sociolinguistic or discourse-related aspects of vocabulary. Immersion teachers focused on vocabulary for the purpose of comprehension more than for drawing explicit attention to the formal and generative properties of words. As a result, immersion students were found to underuse productive prefixes such as 're' in verbs like *recoucher* ("go back to bed"), opting instead for the lexical item *encore* ("again") to express less idiomatically the notion of going back to bed (*coucher encore*) (Harley 1992). Allen et al. recommended more focused learning tasks designed to alert immersion students to differences in the lexical characteristics of their first and second languages as well as more activities designed to increase students' lexical resources. Clipperton (1994) also advocated more explicit vocabulary instruction, recommending experimentation with instructional interventions that integrate explicit vocabulary teaching within a communicative context. In an exploratory study designed to assess more direct techniques for teaching vocabulary in a Grade 11 French immersion class and also in a Grade 9 "extended" French class, Harley, Howard, and Roberge (1996) successfully implemented the following techniques in collaboration with participating teachers: (a) activities involving semantic mapping in which students developed their own vocabulary networks relating to themes such as science fiction and art; (b) activities designed to increase students' awareness of the formal relationship between base words and derived words in the same 'family'. Results showed benefits at both levels, especially for the semantically related vocabulary generated by the semantic networks; students at both grade levels found activities concerning the internal structure of words to be much more challenging.

Reviewing comparisons of incidental and intentional vocabulary learning, Hulstijn (2003) reported that retention rates under intentional learning conditions are much higher than under incidental conditions. This puts into question the popular belief that learners acquire most of their vocabulary incidentally through reading and points instead to an important role for 'depth of processing' in vocabulary retention, but with pros and cons for teachers to weigh:

> For second language educators it is important to note that deep information processing normally requires more time than superficial information processing. Thus, for each device, the benefits must be assessed against the costs. For example, glossing gives a high return in terms of comprehension but a low return in terms of retention, when glossed words appear only once in a text. Retention of glossed words, however, increases substantially when they reoccur several times. On the other hand, retention of words whose meaning has to be inferred may be relatively high, but this benefit comes at the price of time and with the danger of incorrect inferencing (and consequently of learning incorrect meanings) if no corrective feedback is given.   (Hultsijn 2003:364)

Of particular relevance to content-based instruction is that overuse of translation equivalents can serve to reduce depth of processing, thus affecting how well a word is engraved in memory:

> Sometimes a new word is first explained in the foreign language or with pictures, but is then immediately translated in the first language. Pupils will soon realize the pattern of their teacher's explanations and learn that they don't have to concentrate on working out the meaning, because the translation is predictably given afterwards. As a general principle, it would seem useful to avoid translation as a regular way of explaining new words, and to try other techniques, both for variety and for promoting learning. (Cameron 2003:86)

Notwithstanding, Clipperton (1994) referred to several studies to support the inclusion of crosslingual teaching strategies and reference to cognates in vocabulary instruction in immersion and other content-based classrooms (see also Allen et al. 1990). Clipperton (1994) also argued that "the use of context clues to guess unknown words may be a good strategy for inferring meaning but is not always a good strategy for improving lexical proficiency" and recommended that "when new words are first presented, it may be best to do so *out of context*" (p. 743). In the case of young learners, however, Cameron (2003) suggested that they need to hear new words in isolation as well as in a discourse context.

Laufer (2003) recommended the use of word-focused tasks as a means of enabling students to notice and retain vocabulary items more efficiently and more effectively than encountering them only through reading for comprehension. She questioned the ability of second language learners to accurately guess the meaning of new lexical items while reading, and also their ability to then retain the inferred meanings. She cited research indicating that, for learners to recall or recognize the meaning of a word encountered through reading alone, they need to have encountered the word at least ten times (and to have accurately guessed its meaning), and then further require frequent repeated exposures. For this to happen, an inordinate amount of reading needs to take place. For this reason, Laufer recommended word-focused tasks as a more efficient option (see also Laufer 2006), but without undermining the importance of extensive reading for literacy development. Cameron (2003) summed up the importance of repeated exposure even for young learners as follows: "Vocabulary development is not just learning more words but is also importantly about expanding and deepening word knowledge. Children need to meet words again and again, in new contexts that help increase what they know about words. Teaching needs to include the recycling of words" (p. 81).

4.4 Language across the curriculum

Compatible with and often confounded with whole language, language across the curriculum is a curricular approach that emphasizes language development across all content areas of the curriculum. Specifically, it makes a student's language education at school the responsibility of all teachers, regardless of their particular subject area. In this sense, language across the curriculum forms an important strand in Hawkins' (1984) proposal for implementing language awareness programs in middle schools, and continues to be an explicit and primary goal of many ongoing educational reform initiatives. Coordinating support for both target languages across the curriculum in bilingual programs is a key determinant of program effectiveness identified by Corson (1999), who enumerated the main tenants of language across the curriculum as follows:

– language develops mainly through its purposeful use
– learning occurs through talking and writing
– language use contributes to cognitive development

In addition, because of its emphasis on "using language to learn" Day and Shapson (1996) advocated language across the curriculum as the driving force behind effective immersion and content-based approaches.

Language across the curriculum provides a refreshing antidote to the separation of language and content teaching observed in many immersion and content-based classrooms, which should otherwise provide ideal conditions for its implementation. A recent observation study of French and Japanese immersion classrooms reported that, in both settings, "the content-based curriculum was designed to integrate a given theme across all subject-matter instruction at any one time. The teachers were so adept at blurring the borders between language arts classes and subject-matter classes that it was often difficult to identify the type of class under observation" (Lyster & Mori 2006:279). For example, in a Grade 4 combined science and language arts lesson related to the study of local manufacturing and requisite raw materials in science, French immersion students each selected a local manufacturer to write in order to request additional information about its product and the manufacturing process, to be used for follow-up study in class. With emphasis on the final revision stage, just before students each prepared an envelope for mailing their letters, the observed lesson involved a last-minute review as the teacher called on students to ensure they had all included appropriate introductions and conclusions in their letters. As exemplary illustrations of form-focused instruction integrated across the curriculum in timely ways, activities such as these provide purposeful opportunities for strengthening connections between language and content learning.

5. Summary

This chapter has outlined some of the limitations of subject-matter instruction as a means for teaching and learning an additional language, arguing that exposure to only content-based input constrains the communicative abilities of second language learners. Form-focused instruction was proposed as a means for supplementing subject-matter instruction with a view to strengthening language learning objectives and engaging students with language in classrooms where the overriding focus is message-oriented. In lieu of an incidental approach to language instruction, a case was made for a reactive approach to form-focused instruction, because of its propensity for systematic intervention during meaningful interaction, to be used in conjunction with a proactive approach to form-focused instruction, which provides planned intervention without the constraints of brevity and the risk of supplying confusing information. Immersion and content-based classrooms engaged with language across the curriculum provide propitious conditions for teachers to effectively implement form-focused instruction. A systematic focus on language, including attention to grammatical subsystems known to be difficult for classroom learners to acquire through exposure to content alone, can be effectively counterbalanced by more holistic approaches to literacy development, such as whole language, process writing, and language across the curriculum, all of which serve to create a discourse-rich instructional setting.

The research reviewed in this chapter calls for a more intentional and systematic instructional approach to ensure continued language growth in the case of lexical and grammatical development alike, yet with necessary differences between vocabulary and grammar instruction. In the case of vocabulary instruction, a more intentional approach is needed along with some explicit instruction that includes decontextualized analyses of words and their structural properties. In the case of grammar instruction, a more intentional approach is also called for, but with less decontextualized analysis of the target language in terms of its structural parts, and more systematic reference to form/meaning mappings in the target language during meaningful interaction and content-based instruction. The need for somewhat different approaches accounts for what teachers are currently doing as a result of the overriding nature of content-based instruction. That is, because much content instruction is lexically oriented, teachers are naturally inclined to focus on vocabulary for the purpose of comprehension more than for drawing explicit attention to the formal and generative properties of words. At the same time, because content instruction and its lexical orientation do not readily bring grammatical issues to the forefront, teachers are more inclined to do so either incidentally or in a decontextualized manner. Yet researchers strongly recommend less teaching of the formal properties of grammar out of context (e.g., memorizing verb paradigms and parsing sentences) and more attention to the meanings encoded by grammar in communicative contexts. The next chapter focuses on how this can be done through a counterbalanced approach that provides learners with a range of form-focused and content-based opportunities for processing the target language.

CHAPTER 3

Processing language through content

The preceding chapter considered a range of instructional options available to immersion and content-based teachers, narrowing down the most promising options to reactive and proactive form-focused instruction in conjunction with language across the curriculum and other literacy-based approaches. From the perspective of second language learners whose developing interlanguage system engages a range of comprehension and production mechanisms to process language through content, this chapter portrays proactive form-focused instruction as an array of opportunities for noticing, awareness, and practice. The chapter begins by exploring the opportunities that learners have to process language through input. Teachers need to counterbalance instructional strategies that are designed to make content-based input more comprehensible and those designed to make input features more salient. Students in immersion and content-based classrooms benefit from a broad spectrum of repeated opportunities to process language for comprehension as well as for developing their metalinguistic awareness. To complement input-driven instructional techniques, teachers need also to ensure that their students' opportunities to use the second language continue to expand both in quantity and quality. The second half of this chapter illustrates ways in which teachers can provide learners with opportunities to process language through production. An argument is made for counterbalancing these opportunities to ensure target language use in contexts ranging from content-based tasks to more form-focused practice activities.

1. Comprehension

From the beginning, in addition to ensuring the psychological development of their students, one of the primary responsibilities of immersion and content-based teachers is to use the second language in a way that students can easily understand. To ensure comprehension, experienced teachers rely extensively on techniques that transform subject matter into comprehensible input for their students, as described by several researchers and summarized forthwith (see Cloud et al. 2000; Met 1994; Salomone 1992a; Snow 1987; Tardif 1991, 1994).

The goal of teachers throughout any type of content-based program is to enable students to comprehend content presented through the second language. Teachers are known to modify their speech by speaking more slowly in the beginning grades, emphasizing key words or phrases and using cognates, restricted vocabulary, and shorter phrases. They build redundancy into their speech by using discourse modifications such as self-repetition, modeling, and paraphrase (Tardif 1994), as well as multiple examples, definitions, and synonyms to give students many chances to understand the target language. Ideally, teachers provide natural pauses between phrases to give students time to process language and also to give students appropriate "wait time" to interpret questions and formulate responses (Cloud et al. 2000). In tandem with their verbal input, teachers use props, graphs, and other graphic organizers (see Early 2001; Mohan 1986), as well as visual aids such as film, video, and computer or overhead projections. To further facilitate comprehension, teachers rely on extensive body language, including gestures and facial expressions, and a range of paralinguistic elements. Content-based teachers ensure predictability and repetition in instructional routines by using clear boundary markers between activities to orchestrate daily routines in a way that maximizes classroom discipline and opportunities for learning (Mendez 1992; Salomone 1992a). Content-based teachers draw extensively on their students' background knowledge to aid comprehension, and they also draw on students to help one another understand content lessons. Salomone (1992a) observed child-to-child instruction in many immersion classrooms and also noted that teachers sometimes asked students to judge whether other students' responses were correct.

Emphasizing comprehension in this way and to this extent derives in part from Krashen's (1982, 1985, 1994) theory of comprehensible input, according to which the only way for acquisition to occur is when learners are exposed to input containing structures that are a bit beyond their current competence. Krashen claimed that, when input is understood in this way, information about second language syntax is automatically available to the learner, thereby satisfying the prerequisites for its acquisition. Learners are able to understand structures they have not yet acquired because of context and extralinguistic information. Since acquisition results only from comprehensible input and not from conscious learning, according to Krashen, the role of the classroom is to provide plenty of comprehensible input. Because of the emphasis in immersion on comprehensible input conveying subject matter, Krashen (1984) considered it to represent ideal conditions for acquisition, claiming that it may be "the most successful program ever recorded in the professional language-teaching literature" (p. 64).

Instructional techniques that ensure the comprehension of subject matter taught through the medium of the students' second language are at the core of content-based approaches and are requisite for students' academic success. The notion that learners can and should be exposed to language just ahead of their current level of ability, rather than exposed only to language they already know, is essential to immersion and content-based instruction. However, the limits of an exclusively comprehension-based approach to language instruction are now well known, especially in the long-run and for learners aspiring to reach beyond beginner-levels of proficiency and to develop literacy skills in the target language (e.g., Lightbown, Halter, White, & Horst 2002). That is, the continued use of strategies that rely too much on gestures and other visual and non-linguistic support may, over time, have negative effects on the development of students' communicative ability in the second language. Such strategies are unlikely to make the kinds of increasing demands on the learners' language system that Genesee (1987) suggested are necessary for continuous second language learning. For example, Swain (1985) argued that exposure to extensive input via subject-matter instruction engages comprehension strategies that enable students to process language semantically but not necessarily syntactically, allowing them to bypass structural information and to rely instead on pragmatic and situational cues. A helpful example of this was provided by Cameron (2001:40):

> Children listening to a story told in the foreign language from a book with pictures will understand and construct the gist, or outline meaning, of the story in their minds. Although the story may be told in the foreign language, the mental processing does not need to use the foreign language, and may be carried out in the first language or in some language-independent way, using what psychologists call 'mentalese'.

Learners are able to bypass syntax in comprehension of a second language because they can draw instead on "vastly greater stores of schematic and contextual knowledge" (Skehan 1998:26).

Furthermore, although obviously crucial in content-based instruction, instructional techniques that ensure comprehension of subject matter delivered through a second language may be overused at the expense of techniques aimed at developing students' production skills. Weber and Tardif (1991) found that teachers of immersion kindergarten classes used the target language to provide routine cues to encourage participation in classroom rituals but, as expected at this level, did not require children to produce the target language. Instead, teachers tended to expect students to respond by manipulating concrete objects or performing actions such as raising hands, becoming small, curling up, and so on (Tardif 1991). Teachers used the target language also to communicate directly with individual students, focusing on communication and comprehension of the message, but again not on student production. Only in instances of formulaic modeling and vocabulary teaching did teachers expect both comprehension and production. In higher grade levels, Salomone (1992a) found that teachers used several techniques to elicit verbal rather than non-verbal responses, but that students could respond in the language of their choice, "because the language was not a priority; comprehension was" (p. 32). Clearly, teachers need ideally to provide just the right amount of support to make the input comprehensible, while being demanding enough to ensure that learners are actively engaged and learning both language and content from the interaction (Cameron 2001; see also Chapter 4).

Strategies for converting subject matter into comprehensible input represent only the tip of the iceberg in content-based instruction. Hullen and Lentz (1991), for example, argued for instructional strategies designed to reach far beyond mere language comprehension, developing instead students' interpretive skills and their ability to engage in the critical analysis of a wide range of discourse types and genres (see also Cummins 1994; see Schleppegrell, Achugar, & Orteíza 2004, for strategies implemented in high school content-based lessons to develop students' critical analysis of history texts). Netten (1991) argued for a more language-oriented immersion classroom in which teachers would employ as many verbal depictions of meaning as possible in their interactions with children rather than rely on non-verbal connections to facilitate comprehension, even with young learners in Grades 1, 2, and 3. A powerful example of young learners inferring the wrong meaning from their teacher's gestures comes from Weber and Tardif's (1991) study of immersion kindergarten classes. During the daily weather ritual, the teacher usually looked toward the window when asking, "Quel temps fait-il?" (What's the weather like outside?). Many of the children told the researchers that "quel temps fait-il" means "look outside." This came as quite a surprise to the teacher, who had assumed that her students' ability to successfully participate in the daily weather ritual was indicative of more accurate comprehension. The upside of this anecdote is that, after studying the researchers' analysis of the children's difficulty in understanding and producing this utterance, the teacher modified the routine to make it less ambiguous and more meaningful to the children.

There is now considerable theoretical support as well as empirical evidence – much of it from immersion settings – that exposure to comprehensible input alone is insufficient for continued language growth. On the one hand, the emphasis on lexically oriented language learning in content-based instruction bodes well with learners' natural tendency to process language input primarily for meaning and content words. On the other hand, beginning and even intermediate-level learners can skip over redundant grammatical information in order to process input for comprehension, or they can partially process grammatical forms then dump them from working memory in order to free up space for processing lexical items (VanPatten 2004). Harley (1993) argued that "lexically-oriented learning can be seen to be well tuned to the task demands of subject-matter learning where the most pressing need is for global comprehension and for the expression of meaning in context" (p. 62). At the same time, however, "less salient morphosyntactic features of the target system, incongruent with the first language and/or not crucial for comprehension or for getting meaning across may fail to become intake" (Harley 1993:62).

2. Awareness

The need for learners to notice target features in the input, in order to process them as intake, is a crucial first step in second language learning (Schmidt 1990). In order for input to become intake, some degree of noticing must occur, and what gets noticed in the input depends on mediating factors such as prior knowledge and skill, task demands, frequency, and perceptual salience (Gass 1988; Schmidt 1990, 1994). Skehan's (1998) information-processing model identifies conscious awareness of rule-based representations as a key factor in interlanguage development. In his model, noticing plays a central role in converting input to intake during input processing, and is triggered by input qualities such as frequency and salience and by input features that have been contrived for instructional purposes (e.g., typographical enhancement).

Swain (1988, 1996) argued accordingly that content teaching needs to be manipulated and complemented in ways that maximize second language learning, and suggested that, to do so, teachers need to draw students' attention to specific form/meaning mappings by creating contrived contexts that allow students to notice second language features in their full functional range (see also Harley & Swain 1984). However, a basic premise of the information-processing approach to second language learning and use is that learners can devote only so much attention to the various components of complex tasks at one time (McLaughlin & Heredia 1996). Even adult second language learners do not focus on form and meaning simultaneously as they process ambient input (VanPatten 1990). Within meaning-focused contexts, such as content-based classrooms, then, is it reasonable to expect young learners to engage with subject matter and, at the same time, to attend to target forms that are redundant and unnecessary for comprehension?

In the case of young immersion students, it would seem to be the case that they are well equipped for such a challenge. Lambert and Tucker (1972) in their seminal research found that young immersion students developed a "children's version of contrastive linguistics that helps them immeasurably to build vocabulary and to comprehend complex linguistic functions" as well as a linguistic "detective" capacity: "an attentive, patient, inductive concern with words, meanings, and linguistic regularities" (p. 208). Similarly, even the immersion kindergarten children interviewed by Weber and Tardif (1991) enthusiastically volunteered word-for-word translation information, saying, for example, "*les ciseaux* means 'scissors' and *vert* means 'green'" or "*toilette* means 'bathroom' you know." Weber and Tardif interpreted these unsolicited statements as expressions of "genuine delight in a recent discovery that they wished to share," and noted "a sense of pride or joy in their voices as they explained what individual French words meant" (p. 929). With respect to instructional discourse, one of the few strategies used by all immersion teachers observed by Day and Shapson (1996) was "playfulness and experimentation about language" (p. 82), ranging from good-natured reminders about first language interference ("anglicisms") to playing with words and punning. "Because playing with language entails bringing forth language as the object of attention," Day and Shapson (1996) concluded, "perhaps the theme of 'playfulness' could be used by teachers to think about the kinds of things they do to promote language in the classroom, including, but going well beyond, the proverbial classroom language games" (p. 82; see Broner & Tarone 2002, for examples of language play by children in Spanish immersion classrooms).

Since the groundbreaking work of Peal and Lambert (1962), bilingualism has gained the good reputation it deserves as a source of intellectual advantages, even for young children, including greater mental flexibility and greater ability for abstract thinking. Cummins and Swain (1986) reported on various studies of bilingualism showing positive correlations between bilingualism and greater awareness of linguistic operations, arbitrariness in word-referent relationships, and feedback cues (see also Bialystok 2001). Important to mention, however, is that these advantages apply to bilinguals who achieve relatively high threshold levels in both languages. According to Cummins' (2000) threshold hypothesis, aspects of bilingualism that might positively influence cognitive growth and metalinguistic development are unlikely to come into effect until children have attained a certain minimum or threshold level of proficiency in the target language. One can thus expect students' metalinguistic awareness to develop gradually and to become increasingly deployable as they advance through their content-based program.

The extent to which metalinguistic awareness actually contributes to a learner's underlying system of implicit knowledge over time, improving spontaneous language production, is still open to considerable debate. White and Ranta (2002) presented an excellent summary of the wide range of positions that researchers have posited to exist between metalinguistic performance and oral production. In their own empirical study of the use of possessive determiners by intensive ESL learners in Grade 6, they demonstrated a relationship between the students' performance on metalinguistic tasks and their performance in spontaneous oral production. White and Ranta cautioned, however, that similar results might not necessarily obtain with other target features nor in other instructional settings. While there might not always be a direct relationship between metalinguistic awareness and its influence during online production, it is argued here that, in the case of immersion and content-based classrooms, metalinguistic awareness has the potential to serve students as an indispensable tool for extracting linguistic information from meaning-oriented input and thus for learning language through subject-matter instruction. That is, young learners in content-based classrooms will benefit from the inclusion of age-appropriate noticing and awareness activities that enable them to draw on their linguistic sensitivity in a way that primes them for the kind of implicit analysis of naturalistic input they need to engage in to drive their interlanguage development forward (see Ranta 2002; Skehan 1998). Moreover, because young learners in immersion classrooms rely heavily on the use of formulaic chunks in their early production (e.g., Weber & Tardif 1991), teachers can exploit their students' emerging metalinguistic awareness to engage increasingly over time in analyses of formulaic items as a means of developing a more generative rule-based system. The intent, of course, is not to overload young learners with metalinguistic information, because this would be at odds with the overall content-based approach.

Teachers in immersion and content-based classrooms can draw on the incipient metalinguistic awareness that accompanies their students' burgeoning bilingualism as a means of priming them to notice target features in the mainly content-based input. At least two phases are required for learners to notice target features in a manner robust enough to make the forms available as intake: a noticing phase and an awareness phase. Rather than distinguishing noticing from awareness, Ellis (2002) referred to two different types of awareness: (a) awareness of formal properties of the target language that are consciously noticed, and (b) awareness in the sense of developing an explicit representation of the target form (see also Schmidt 1990). In order to depict a range of tasks that can be designed to make forms appear more salient, a distinction is made in this book between *noticing* activities and *awareness* activities, parallel with Ellis's characterization of two types of awareness, but with a disclaimer to acknowledge that, in practice, the distinction is not entirely categorical. Generally speaking, learners engage primarily in receptive processing during noticing activities, which serve to move the learner towards more target-like representations of the second language. Learners engage either receptively or productively, or both, in awareness activities, which serve to consolidate the cognitive restructuring of rule-based declarative representations. Noticing and awareness activities together comprise what Leow (2007) referred to as receptive practice, which aims "to promote robust input processing leading to subsequent internalization of the linguistic data in the input" (p. 21). They entail what VanPatten (1996) called structured input: "activities in which learners are given the opportunity to process form in the input in a 'controlled' situation so that better form-meaning connections might happen compared with what might happen in less controlled situations" (p. 60). Such activities serve to initiate the transition from implicit to explicit knowledge of the target language (Bialystok 1994) and to anchor it solidly in students' consciousness to ensure easy access during language use (DeKeyser 1998).

Noticing activities serve as catalysts for drawing learners' attention to problematic target features that have been contrived to appear more salient and/or frequent in oral and written input. Various ways of making target forms more salient in the input and, therefore, more readily noticed by learners were proposed by Sharwood Smith (1993) under the rubric of "input enhancement." In the case of written input, input enhancement includes typographical enhancement such as colour coding or boldfacing, and, in the case of oral input, intonational stress and gestures. Awareness activities require learners to do more than merely notice enhanced forms in the input and instead to engage in some degree of elaboration (Sharwood Smith 1981, 1993). Such elaboration may include inductive rule-discovery tasks and opportunities to compare and contrast language patterns, followed by different types of metalinguistic information. In some cases, the contrasted patterns may entail differences between the first and second language. For example, a technique used by the immersion teachers observed by Day and Shapson (1996) was the exploitation of their students' first language knowledge as a resource for using the target language. In classroom settings where learners share the same first language, several studies confirm that they use their first language to complete collaborative tasks, inciting some researchers to explore the benefits of using and/or referring to the first language in second language learning and teaching (e.g., Cook 2001; DiCamilla & Anton 1997; Swain & Lapkin 2000; Turnbull 2001; Turnbull & Arnett 2002). Although focusing on differences between the first and second language has not been standard practice in immersion classrooms, Harley (1993:250) argued that "teacher-guided cross-lingual comparisons could help clarify some second language distinctions for immersion students, especially where partial similarities have encouraged an assumption of complete identity between first and second language items" (see also Spada & Lightbown 1999; Spada et al. 2005).

Noticing activities involving input enhancement alone are insufficient without follow-up awareness activities that include rule-discovery tasks or the provision of metalinguistic information. In her study of the effects of typographical input enhancement on the acquisition of possessive determiners by francophone learners of English in Grade 6, White (1998) concluded that students would have benefited from more explicit information than that made available through enhanced input alone. In a subsequent study by Spada et al. (2005), students provided with metalinguistic information in the form of a "rule of thumb" about possessive determiners indeed performed better. Similarly, in her study of the effects of instruction on the acquisition of past tenses, Harley (1989) concluded that students would have made more significant progress had they been provided with metalinguistic information about the formal properties of the two tenses.

The instructional treatments in the intervention studies designed by Day and Shapson (1991), Harley (1989, 1998), Lyster (1994a, 2004a), and Wright (1996) used a range of noticing and awareness activities to promote the perception of problematic target features in a variety of genres including curriculum materials, legends, letters, invitations, novels, songs, rhyming verses, games, crossword puzzles, and word searches. For example, in Harley's (1989) study of the effects of instruction on the acquisition by Grade 6 immersion students of perfective and imperfective past tenses in French, students began by reading a traditional legend about were-wolves. The legend had been enhanced in the sense that past tense forms occurred frequently and the functional distinctions between the two tenses were made salient by the narrative. Then students were asked to identify the two different past tenses in the text and, based on the narrative, to infer the different functions of each tense. In yet another activity, students were asked to compare several pairs of pictures, the first depicting a completed action and the second depicting an incomplete action, labelled appropriately (e.g., *The pilot was opening his parachute* vs. *The pilot had opened his parachute*). Students were then asked to create and illustrate their own sentences to contrast completed and incomplete actions, labelling them appropriately. In Wright's (1996) instructional treatment targeting verbs of motion with student in Grade 4/5, the teacher read aloud to students a series of short books each replete with target verbs. After each book, the teacher explicitly drew students' attention to the target verbs by means of a chart and initiated discussion of their precise meanings and possible occurrence with prepositions. The teacher also pointed out to students their tendency to use a high-coverage verb plus a prepositional phrase rather than one of the target verbs. After writing on the blackboard what students typically say (e.g., *Il va en bas de la colline*), the teacher elicited from students the more target-like use of '*Il descend la colline*'. In addition to various follow-up exercises and in order to create a more meaningful context for students to notice the target verbs, a game was played during several physical education lessons in which students adopted the roles of predators and prey. Explanations of the role of the animals and the rules of the game were replete with target verbs.

In Lyster (1994a), the instructional materials designed to improve students' sociolinguistic competence consisted of noticing activities that required students to classify utterances as either formal or informal. The awareness tasks then required them to contrast the language items that actually make utterances either formal or informal. Students were first asked to notice these contrasts in their first language, using examples adapted from Astley and Hawkins (1985). Various ways of greeting and leave-taking, as well as introducing people, were then presented in their second language, and students were asked to identify, with justification, the level of formality of each utterance. In addition, students compared formal and informal versions of letters and invitations to identify stylistically appropriate target language features. Activities were also designed around dialogues extracted from a novel that required students to notice and then explain differences in second-person pronominal reference. This awareness task was ranked the highest by students for its relevance and applicability (Lyster 1998e), pointing to the potential for using literature (i.e., dialogues from plays and novels) as an effective means for increasing students' awareness of sociolinguistic variation. Students were also asked to reflect on the way they themselves use second-person pronouns with their current and past immersion teachers, and to imagine, if they were francophone, how they would address their friends' parents and other teachers in the school.

In Harley's (1998) study with Grade 2 immersion students learning about grammatical gender, noticing activities required students to attend to the co-occurrence of nouns with gender-specific articles on identification labels displayed around the classroom. Several listening activities were designed to provide students with opportunities to listen for articles and noun endings. For example, in games such as 'Simon Says' students stood up or touched their toes when they heard nouns with masculine endings and squatted or touched their head when they heard feminine endings. Students were read a Halloween story and, on the second reading, were asked to listen for and identify masculine and feminine words. Similarly, while listening to a recorded song, they were asked to listen for words with a particular ending. Crossword puzzles and word searches provided further opportunities for students to notice target nouns with characteristic masculine or feminine endings. Awareness activities required students each to create their own gender-specific dictionary, to which they added new target vocabulary from each week's activities. They also completed various exercises requiring them to match rhyming words to which they then assigned gender-specific determiners. A game of 'Concentration' was created so that students had to match pictures of nouns that had same-sounding endings. The game evolved each week to include new vocabulary and new sets of target endings. For further practice in associating nouns with grammatical gender, the game 'I Spy' was played so that the student giving the clues had to say whether the word was masculine or feminine.

Harley found that the most successful activities were those most closely associated with themes that teachers were emphasizing in their regular curriculum. More difficult was exposing young learners to lots of new vocabulary unrelated to the curriculum. In particular, the words used in the various games that focused on noun endings were formally but not semantically linked, and this was found to be problematic in the theme-based Grade 2 curriculum. To overcome this problem in grammatical gender activities for Grade 5 students in Lyster's (2004a) study, the form-focused instructional activities were embedded in the children's regular curriculum materials, which integrated language arts, history, and science into monthly dossiers. To accompany the dossier for the month of February, the research team created a student workbook that contained simplified versions of texts found in the regular curriculum materials, in which noticing activities were embedded for the purpose of drawing students' attention to noun endings as predictors of grammatical gender. The endings of target nouns had been highlighted in bold and students were asked to fill in the missing definite or indefinite article before each noun. The first set of activities revolved around the founding of Quebec City, as illustrated by the following extract:

> *Québec ressemblait de plus en plus à _____ vrai <u>village</u>, doté notamment de _____ deuxième <u>habitation</u> de Champlain, d' _____ <u>chapelle</u>, d' _____ <u>magasin</u> et d'autres bâtiments. Sur _____ <u>plateau</u> au-dessus du cap Diamant, il y avait un fort, quelques maisons et _____ petite <u>église</u> avec son presbytère.*

Students had to classify target nouns according to their endings and to indicate whether nouns with these endings were masculine or feminine. This format was repeated with texts about the founding of Montreal and Trois-Rivières, and yet again in a True/False exercise about the founding of all three colonies. Students were then given a list of new nouns, which had not appeared in any previous exercises, and were asked to indicate the grammatical gender of each, by adding the right article, based on what they had noticed in previous activities, and then to suggest rules for determining the gender of these nouns. Similar exercises ensued, so there was considerable repetitiveness inherent in these activities although they were always related to the students' subject-matter instruction.

Students were also exposed to songs and rhyming verses to draw their attention to noun endings and the role they play in gender attribution. The following verse is extracted from a fanciful poem that was used as a springboard for students, first, to infer that nouns ending in -*ine* are feminine and, second, to create their own rhyming verses:

> *Dans ma maison, au fond de la cuisine,*
> *Il se trouve une chose, une drôle de machine.*
> *Un peu comme un bol mais moins grosse qu'une piscine,*
> *On y mélange plein de choses, toujours avec de la farine.*

To help students create their own rhyming verses, a set of laminated posters, one for each targeted noun ending and each listing many high-frequency nouns with that particular ending, had been placed around each classroom to serve as a quick reference for students throughout the instructional unit. In addition, the teachers provided feedback to further increase their students' awareness of gender attribution in their oral production; the effects of the different feedback treatments will be revisited in Chapter 4.

3. Production

Student production in the target language becomes increasingly important in content-based instruction as students interact with teachers, with peers, and with the content itself. Allen et al. (1990) found that opportunities for sustained talk by students, however, were infrequent in immersion classrooms (see also Genesee 1991). Fewer than 15% of student turns in the second language were more than a clause in length and this represented a considerably smaller proportion of the sustained speech observed during the portion of the day devoted to instruction in the students' first language. Swain (1988) concluded accordingly that typical content teaching does not provide extensive opportunities for student production. In light of (a) the input-based instructional approach associated with content teaching, (b) observations of minimal production by students, and (c) their low levels of grammatical competence, Swain (1993) proposed the output hypothesis: "Through producing language, either spoken or written, language acquisition/learning may occur" (p. 159). Although Krashen (1994, 1998) has maintained his position that language production plays no role in language acquisition, extensive use of the second language as a means of developing second language proficiency resonates well with many language teachers. In fact, Salomone (1992a) and Day and Shapson (1996) both reported having observed considerably more opportunities for immersion students to engage in extended language production than the minimal amount reported by Allen et al. (1990).

The output hypothesis is compatible with skill acquisition theory, which attributes an important role to practice. Opportunity for practice as a means of developing fluency, however, is only one of the roles attributed to output by Swain (1993, 1995), who identified three others. First, output pushes learners to move from semantic processing to syntactic processing and, as a result, to notice what they do not know or know only partially. When learners notice a gap between what they need to say and what they know how to say, they can respond in one of three ways: (a) ignore the gap; (b) identify the gap and pay attention to relevant input; or (c) search their own linguistic knowledge for information that might help close the gap by generating new knowledge or consolidating existing knowledge. Second, output has a metalinguistic function that enables learners to use language in order to reflect on language. Third, as learners stretch their interlanguage to meet communicative needs, they use output as a way of testing hypotheses about new language forms and structures (see also Pica, Holliday, Lewis, & Morgenthaler 1989). During interaction with others, learners modify their output, and more specifically through external feedback provided by teachers or peers (or through internal feedback), learners are able to "reprocess" their output in ways that reveal the "leading edge" of their interlanguage (Swain 1995:131; see Swain 2005, for a summary of research related to the output hypothesis).

3.1 Content-based tasks

Content-based instruction is thought to provide ideal contexts for second language learning to occur naturally, because of the countless opportunities for authentic and purposeful use of the target language generated by the study of subject matter (Snow et al. 1989). Genesee (1987) argued that the academic curriculum stimulates language development by placing increasingly high levels of cognitive and linguistic demands on students. He proposed academic (i.e., content-based) tasks themselves, rather than a language-based syllabus, as a basis for stimulating second language development, but added that "maximum language learning in immersion will probably result only to the extent that the curriculum exploits opportunities for discourse in the service of academic achievement." He proposed a process approach to second language pedagogy whereby "certain interactional processes of a discoursal nature," hypothesized to contribute to language development, are instantiated in academic tasks, which in turn govern the actual units of language to be learned: "It follows that second language learning will then proceed in response to the communication demands of academic work, given certain motivational conditions" (p. 176).

The argument that second language development will be driven primarily by the discourse in which students need to engage to complete academic tasks is premised on the theoretical assumption that communicative language ability is acquired through purposeful communication. Not accounted for, however, are research findings that have documented the ineffectiveness of immersion for promoting levels of accuracy that match its success in developing fluency (Wesche & Skehan 2002). One solution is to incorporate Cummins' (1981, 1986, 2000) well-known developmental framework as a guideline for sequencing academic tasks in a way that increasingly makes them more cognitively demanding and, at the same time, more context-reduced in order to push students to extend their linguistic resources.

As seen in Figure 1, Cummins' framework accounts for a range of contextual support and different degrees of cognitive involvement as students engage in academic tasks. At the context-embedded end of the communication continuum, a wide range of meaningful interpersonal and paralinguistic cues provide

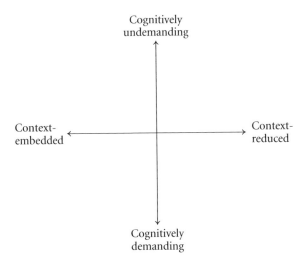

Figure 1. Range of contextual support and degree of cognitive involvement in academic tasks (Cummins 2000:68)

students with the support necessary for them to successfully complete a task. At the other end of the continuum, to participate in context-reduced communication, students need to rely primarily on linguistic cues to meaning, and thus successful completion of the task is contingent on students' engagement with language itself. The vertical axis in Cummins' model refers to the cognitive load required for task completion. At one end of the spectrum, cognitively undemanding tasks are those in which the linguistic tools have become largely automatized and, thus, require little active cognitive involvement for task completion. At the other end, cognitively demanding tasks are those in which the linguistic tools have not become automatized and, thus, require active cognitive involvement for successful task completion. Cummins (2000:69) argued that, as students progress through the grades, "they are increasingly required to manipulate language in cognitively demanding and context-reduced situations that differ significantly from everyday conversational interactions." See Cloud et al. (2000:127) for excellent ideas on how to vary strategies for teaching content in accordance with increasing levels of second language proficiency across grade levels.

In much current SLA research, task-based instruction has increasingly gained popularity as a theoretically sound way of organizing communicative language teaching (Bygate, Skehan, & Swain 2001; Ellis 2003; Skehan 1998; Willis 1996). A commonly accepted definition of a task is that (a) meaning is primary, (b) there is a goal to work towards or a communication problem to solve, (c) there is relationship with real-world activities, and (d) assessment is in terms of outcomes (e.g., Ellis 2000; Skehan 1998; Nunan 1989). Typical tasks observed and documented by research include the following: diagramming and giving instructions about how to lay out a pegboard; picture description tasks in which one learner describes a picture to another learner who must draw the picture; jigsaw tasks in which learners construct a story by exchanging information about their own individually held pictures of the story; and various other information-gap exercises and "spot-the-difference" tasks (e.g., Pica 2000; Pica, Kanagy, & Falodun 1993; Skehan 1998). One may well wonder to what extent students actually view such tasks as related to the real world. Williams and Burden (1997) characterized tasks used in communicative language classrooms to exchange information in this way as "meaningful" but not "purposeful," because they lack educational purpose and thus fall short of empowering students. Defining task broadly as "any activity that learners engage in to further the process of learning a language" (p. 168), Williams and Burden (1997) suggested that tasks for school-age learners can be made purposeful by investing them with an educational rationale, such as the development of thinking skills, problem-solving skills, and learning how to learn. Because academic tasks undertaken in immersion and content-based classrooms typically aim to engage students with subject matter, they are invested ipso facto with educational purpose. Consider the following science and geography tasks observed by the author in Grade 8 immersion classrooms:

–   To demonstrate their understanding of how geographical phenomena determine meteorological events, students were asked to create a continent, identifying its name and illustrating its geographical features on a map, which they then presented to their teacher and classmates with a detailed explanation of how the various geographical features influence the continent's overall climatic conditions.

–   To apply their knowledge of the relationship between weight distribution and equilibrium, students each created a hanging mobile made of string and dowel adorned with various objects brought from home. Students weighed objects, measured distance, and used algebraic formulae to determine the exact fulcrum points in order to ensure equal weight distribution and a perfectly balanced hanging mobile.

Content-based tasks such as these are designed to create opportunities for in-depth understanding and for learning by doing. Effective content teaching is generally considered to include hands-on tasks that engage learners in experiences such as these. At the same time, the creation of a mobile in science or a map of a student-designed continent in geography, with the support of concrete materials and graphic aids, are strategically designed to be cognitively demanding but context-embedded and, therefore, are unlikely to push learners to extend their productive repertoire in oral expression. These tasks fit well with what are considered best practices in content instruction as it unfolds in immersion and other content-based classrooms, but are limited if associated only with oral expression. Therefore, content-based tasks need also to include a written component designed to be context-reduced so that learners are required to use the target language for academic purposes without the contextual support that normally scaffolds oral interaction.

Tasks that emphasize oral fluency and creativity, and that vary in scope and structure to accommodate different traditions across various content areas, may provide a poor context for developing language skills (Bygate 1999; Ellis 2000). In achieving fluency by ignoring accuracy or by concentrating on a narrow repertoire of language, learners do not necessarily extend and refine their interlanguage system. Even in the tasks used in Harley's (1989) and Day and Shapson's (1991) interventions, which were specifically designed to encourage the productive use of specific target forms during oral interaction (i.e., the creation of childhood albums and the design of futuristic space colonies), target forms were avoided and superseded by spontaneous expression and the concomitant use of simplified forms. Day and Shapson (1991) observed a tendency during oral tasks for students to use the present tense as they interacted together in groups, avoiding the conditional and thereby decreasing their use of conditionals in a meaningful context. As Ellis (2000) argued, "It cannot be assumed that achieving communicative effectiveness in the performance of a task will set up the interactive conditions that promote second language acquisition" (p. 213).

3.2 Form-focused tasks

Given the difficulty inherent in implementing tasks that simultaneously focus learners' attention on both communication and form, some researchers have turned their attention to collaborative tasks designed specifically to draw learners' attention to form. A growing number of studies of learner-learner dyads in second language classrooms have shown that when learners work collaboratively to complete tasks with a linguistic focus they engage in "meta-talk" in which they "use language to reflect on language use" (Swain 1998:68). For example, Kowal and Swain (1994) presented a study of Grade 8 French immersion students working in pairs to complete a "dictogloss" (Wajnryb 1990), a text reconstruction task designed to encourage students to reflect on their own output, and described by Kowal and Swain (1994: 10) as follows:

> a short, dense text is read to the learners at normal speed; while it is being read, students jot down familiar words and phrases; the learners work together in small groups to reconstruct the text from their shared resources; and the various versions are then analyzed and compared in a whole class setting.

Based on the interactions recorded while students worked in pairs to reconstruct their texts, Kowal and Swain proposed that the task allowed students to "notice the gap" between what they wanted to say and what they were able to say, which in turn led them to make language form the topic of their discussions as they worked collaboratively to fill the gap. Students formed hypotheses, which they tested out against the dictionary, the teacher, and each other. Kowal and Swain concluded that this type of collaborative task (a) allowed for reflection and better understanding, which led to the creation of new knowledge and the consolidation of existing knowledge, and (b) encouraged learners to move from the semantic processing dominant in comprehension to the syntactic processing needed for production. Swain and Lapkin (1998, 2001, 2002) as well investigated the use of collaborative writing tasks and their potential for encouraging immersion students to use language as a means for reflecting metalinguistically on their use of the target language. They demonstrated that students use language in this way as they complete dictogloss and jigsaw tasks. Swain and Lapkin concluded that the writing component common to both tasks was an important factor in encouraging students to focus on form. In addition, through analysis of think-aloud protocols with immersion students about their writing, Swain and Lapkin (1995) found that the students' oral output, as they thought aloud, triggered noticing and led them to attend to grammatical form, which in turn, they suggested, provided propitious opportunities for language learning to take place.

Lyster (1993, 1994b) explored collaborative jigsaw tasks as a means of integrating a focus on language in the experiential context of immersion classrooms. Jigsaw used as a collaborative learning task differs substantially from Jigsaw communication tasks, which are employed in studies of negotiation for meaning to provide a context for learners to use various conversational moves to exchange information. Jigsaw learning tasks entail *home groups* consisting of four members, each of whom also belongs to a different *expert group*. Members of each expert group specialize in a particular area of expertise, and then return to their home groups to share what they have learned (see Heller, Barker,

& Lévy 1989). In Lyster's study, a weeklong project consisting of daily tasks was designed to consolidate students' awareness of differences between formal and informal uses of French as well as between spoken and written French. The tasks were designed to enable students to discover and apply stylistic differences through a project undertaken in groups of four following the jigsaw approach to cooperative learning

The project began on Day 1 with a whole-class presentation of four texts, all conveying the same message – how to operate an audiocassette recorder – in four distinct ways: formal speech, informal speech, formal writing, and informal writing. Students were asked to guess possible contexts for each text (who is speaking to whom, where, and why?) and to describe differences in language use. Then in groups of four, which were to become the home groups in the jigsaw, students completed exercises about different vocabulary and expressions used in the four texts. In order to form expert groups for the next activity, each member of the home group chose one of four areas of expertise: formal speech, informal speech, formal writing, or informal writing. On Day 2, students were presented a second series of four different texts expressing the same message (i.e., how to prepare chocolate mousse). After comparing the texts in their expert groups, focusing on the texts reflecting their group's expertise, students returned to their home groups to evaluate their work by referring to answers found by other experts in the home group. (The task was designed so that the evaluation of its outcomes required mutual interdependence among home-group members.) On Days 3 and 4, each home group met to work on a theme of their choice which they had to convey through formal and informal written texts and formal and informal spoken texts to be audio-recorded. On Day 5, each group made a class presentation, which, along with explanations of how each text represented a particular register, addressed the following topics: giving directions in Quebec City, presenting classroom rules, selling a car, ordering items from a department store, preparing a banana split, making microwave popcorn, and baking chocolate chip cookies. The final products aptly illustrated what Swain (1985, 1995) meant by comprehensible output: precise and appropriate uses of the second language that stretched learners to the leading edge of their interlanguage resources – without recourse to paralinguistic cues and over-reliance on all-purpose lexical items of general meaning that otherwise recur frequently in immersion students' production as they negotiate for meaning in context (Harley 1992, 1993).

Still other research has shown that during dyadic communication tasks that have not necessarily been designed to call attention to form, adult learners themselves may draw attention to language (e.g., McDonough & Mackey

2000; Williams 1999), although many studies still claim a pivotal role for teachers to intervene in timely ways that draw attention to wrong hypotheses and non-target output (Swain 1998; Williams 1999; Samuda 2001). Storch (2002) found that some types of dyads are more successful than others (see also Foster 1998; Iwashita 2001), concluding that "learners, when working in pairs, can scaffold each other's performance, yet such scaffolding is more likely to occur when pairs interact in a certain pattern: either collaborative or expert/novice" (Storch 2002:147). Similarly, Kowal and Swain (1997) found that students in homogeneous dyads collaborated better than those in heterogeneous dyads. In addition, Naughton (2006) argued that "small group oral interaction does not necessarily yield language-learning opportunities or encourage their exploitation" (p. 171), because, depending on degrees of motivation and homogeneity across first language backgrounds, learners in small groups can engage in "interaction that is comprehensible to all, yet severely limited in terms of interlanguage development" (p. 179). Naughton found, though, that teachers are in a position to intervene to "shape patterns of interaction in an attempt to maximize the creation and exploitation of learning opportunities" and can do so through strategy training designed to encourage students to engage in meta-talk and to "reflect on their discourse in a metacognitive way" (p. 179). Ranta and Lyster (2007) argued, however, that collaborative tasks engaging learners in meta-talk characterized by some degree of metalinguistic analysis, such as those employed by Swain, Kowal, Lapkin, and Lyster, are unlikely to result in higher levels of grammatical accuracy in learners' spontaneous oral production. This is because, as posited by the theory of transfer-appropriate learning, "the expression of previous learning will be successful to the extent that the learners' psychological state existing at the time of learning matches that required at the time of expression" (Segalowitz 1997:105). In other words, optimal conditions favouring the assimilation of second language knowledge into a learner's implicit system, and thus available in spontaneous production and not only for monitoring purposes, should ideally include processing that resembles the processing that will occur when learning is to be put to use. This brings us now to the role of production practice.

3.3 Skill acquisition through practice

Practice gets a raw deal in the field of applied linguistics. Most laypeople simply assume that practice is a necessary condition for language learning, without giving the concept much further thought, but many applied linguists eschew the term 'practice'. For some, the word conjures up images of mind-numbing drills in the sweatshops of foreign language learning, while for others it means fun and games to appease students on Friday afternoon. Practice is by no means a dirty word in other domains of human endeavor, however. Parents dutifully take their kids to soccer practice, and professional athletes dutifully show up for team practice, sometimes even with recent injuries. Parents make their kids practice their piano skills at home, and the world's most famous performers of classical music often practice for many hours a day, even if it makes their fingers hurt. If even idolized, spoiled, and highly paid celebrities are willing to put up with practice, why not language learners, teachers, or researchers?   (DeKeyser 2007: 1)

Notwithstanding the alleged reluctance of applied linguists to embrace practice activities as an essential component of second language instruction, researchers in immersion settings have been advocating the importance of both receptive and production practice activities for years (e.g., Harley & Swain 1984). In their observation study of immersion classrooms, Allen et al. (1990) reported that the "speech acts which occur naturally in the classroom context may provide little opportunity for students to produce the full range of target language forms" (p. 74) and recommended that teachers implement "carefully planned and guided communicative practice that will push students towards the production of comprehensible output" (p. 76). They continued:

> One form of guidance is to engage students in activities, contrived by the teacher to focus attention on potential problems, that will naturally elicit particular uses of language. Another form of guidance is to develop activities that make use of functions which would otherwise rarely be encountered in the classroom.   (p. 76)

DeKeyser's (1998, 2001, 2007) work in this area, including his recent volume titled *Practicing for second language use: Perspectives from applied linguistics and cognitive psychology*, goes a long way in increasing our understanding of the role of practice in second language learning. He acknowledged much confusion about what is meant by practice, owing to its wide range of definitions: "the narrow sense of repeated narrowly-focused exercises to optimize retrieval of what one has learned, or the slightly wider sense of any kind of second language use that will encourage expansion and fine-tuning of existing knowledge, to the widest sense of any kind of contact with the second language that will improve knowledge of it at some level" (DeKeyser 2007: 289). DeKeyser (1998) broadly defined practice as "engaging in an activity with the goal of becoming better at it" (p. 50) and more specifically in reference to second language learning as "specific activities in the second language, engaged in systematically, deliberately, with the goal of developing knowledge of and skills in the second language" (DeKeyser 2007:1). Whereas Lightbown (1985, 2000) presented convincing arguments that practice "does not make perfect," Muñoz (2007) suggested that "it does make better" (p. 229).

While the concern earlier in this chapter was with receptive practice through noticing and awareness activities, the focus here is on production practice. Cognitive theory, as outlined in Chapter 1, posits that practice is essential to skill acquisition because it provides learners with opportunities to proceduralise their declarative knowledge. In this sense, language production is part of learning rather than only an outcome (cf. Krashen 1994). An alternative view of skill acquisition is Logan's (1988) instance theory, whereby automatization involves, not the proceduralization of rule-based representations with increasingly less attention, but rather a transition from rule-based performance to memory-based performance (see DeKeyser 2001; Robinson & Ha 1993; Schmidt 1992, 2001). In this view, procedures initially deriving from rule-based representations become available as memory-based chunks, which then operate autonomously. With minimal computational demands, retrieval from the memory-based system involves more efficient processing, enables fluent performance, and is thus considered synonymous with automaticity.

To account more specifically for second language learning and variability in second language performance, still from an information-processing perspective, Skehan (1998) described a dual-coding system, which reconciles both rule-based and memory-based systems as equally important representational systems for language learners. Output processing engages the learner's memory capacity differentially through retrieval from the dual-mode system, composed of two interrelated representational systems: an analytic rule-based system and a memory-driven exemplar-based system (see also Murphy 2000). Retrieval for the purpose of production thus leads either to computed rule-based performance or memory-driven exemplar-based performance. Skehan argued that, during online communication, communicative pressure and the need for fast access will make the exemplar-based system the system of choice, thus reducing the likelihood that the compact storage and powerful generative rules of the rule-based system will be accessed to compute well-formed utterances. Skehan argued that interlanguage change is more effectively activated through the rule-based system and that conscious awareness predisposes learners towards such a rule-based perspective (see also Schmidt 1990).

These two representational systems, however, are not entirely separate; Skehan (1998) considered them to be "in constant dialectic" (p. 92), enabling learners to engage in complementary processes of analysis and synthesis (see also Klein 1986):

> On the one hand, the learner needs to be prepared to focus on structure, and to identify pattern. On the other, the identification of pattern is, in itself, insufficient, because the fruits of such analysis need to be reintegrated and synthesized into fluent performance with the patterns concerned. . . . The analysis is necessary to enable the learner to gain generativity and flexibility, and the synthesis is necessary to enable fluency and control to be achieved. But each must be ready to be used continually during an individual's course of language development.   (Skehan 1998:92)

Similarly, Ellis (2003) suggested that production might be the mechanism that connects the learner's dual systems, "enabling movement to occur from the memory-based to the rule-based system and vice-versa. If this interpretation is correct, learners may not be so reliant on input as has been generally assumed in SLA. They may be able to utilize their own internal resources, via using them in production, to both construct and complexify their interlanguages" (Ellis 2003:115).

In pedagogical terms, the dual-coding system implies two different types of production practice, both of which are beneficial, but for different purposes: controlled practice and communicative practice. The distinction between controlled and communicative practice activities parallels Ellis's (2003) distinction between *focused* production tasks (i.e., tasks that elicit specific language features) and *unfocused* production tasks (i.e., tasks designed to elicit general samples of learner language). The distinction also parallels Loschky and Bley-Vroman's (1993) distinction between *task-essentialness*, which prevents the successful completion of a task unless the elicited structure is used, and *task-naturalness*, whereby the elicited structure may arise naturally but the task can easily be completed without it. In terms of Cummins' model (see Figure 1), production practice needs to be cognitively undemanding, roughly speaking, to enable learners to focus more readily on language. Controlled practice tends to be context-reduced, while communicative practice tends to be context-embedded. At one end of the practice spectrum, controlled practice activities engage learners' awareness of rule-based representations and are thus useful for circumventing their over-reliance on communication strategies and effecting change in the interlanguage (Ranta & Lyster 2007). At the other end of the practice spectrum, communicative practice activities engage learners in more open-ended and meaning-focused tasks with fewer constraints to ensure accuracy, thus proving effective for promoting confidence and motivation to use the second language, and for providing a safe playing field for students to try out communication strategies. Because they encourage quick access to lexicalized exemplar-based representations that facilitate spontaneous production, communicative practice activities, however, do not engage learners' language awareness to the same extent, thereby reducing the potential for changes to the interlanguage system (Skehan 1998).

Lyster (2004b) found that, in cases where the areas of linguistic difficulty were sources of persistent errors for immersion students, controlled practice was more effective than communicative practice. However, Segalowitz (2000) argued that second language fluency develops as a result of practice that has not only been extensive and repetitive, thus building automaticity, but that has also been genuinely communicative in nature and therefore transfer-appropriate. A revealing example of how difficult it is for children to transfer skills that have been automatized in a controlled production activity to a more communicative context comes to us from immersion kindergarten classrooms where Weber and Tardif (1991) reported that some children in their study had difficulty in a context of interaction to retrieve certain phrases they had learned through songs. Some children literally had to go through the song, as they enacted the accompanying gestures, in search of the appropriate second language phrase. "Each time they wanted to use the phrase, they had to start the song from the beginning even if the target phrase was at the end. One girl, moreover, could only sing, not state the phrase." The researchers concluded that songs were "helpful sources of modeling but the children seemed to require additional spoken practice in other contexts to free themselves of a dependency on gestures and rote memory" (p. 928).

To promote second language learning, therefore, practice activities, whether considered controlled or communicative, need to involve the processing of words and formulae for communicative purposes. Designing practice activities that are both controlled (in the sense of requiring use of specific target forms) and communicative in purpose, however, is no small undertaking. An excellent example of both is evident in the content-driven activities used in Doughty and Varela's (1998) classroom study, which took place in a content-based ESL science class, targeting the simple past and the conditional past in the context of science experiments. A group of 11–14-year-old students conducted a set of experiments in accordance with their regular science curriculum. To report their results accurately, they needed to use the simple past and the conditional past. For example, in one of the experiments, students were asked first to make the following prediction: "Which will go farthest across a desk when blown: a plastic cup with three pennies, one with six pennies, one with nine pennies, or one with twelve pennies?" After completing the experiment, students produced a written lab report and were also questioned orally about their experiments. They were asked to recount the procedure they followed to complete the experiment and also to report the results, thus creating an obligatory context for use of the past tense. In addition, they were asked to recall their initial prediction (e.g., "I thought the cup with three pennies would go the farthest") as well as what the teacher had predicted, thus creating obligatory and purposeful contexts for using and re-using both the simple past and the conditional past during subject-matter lessons. What follows now is a selective summary of practice activities implemented in the aforementioned immersion classroom intervention studies, to illustrate other attempts at designing practice conditions that range from controlled to communicative.

The creation of childhood albums was a pivotal activity in the treatment materials used in Harley's (1989) study targeting perfective and imperfective past tenses. Designed with a personalized theme to motivate students to use the second language, this activity required students to describe various childhood memories, both orally and in writing along with authentic photographs, depicting either specific and completed actions or ongoing and incomplete actions in the past. Each student's album concluded with five questions about his or her past that the student was then asked by a classmate during an oral interview that was audio recorded so that other students could listen to it later. Games occurred as well in Harley's study, creating opportunities for students to practice using the imperfective past tense in appropriate contexts. For example, one student mimed an action to the whole class while another was out of the classroom. The student returning to the classroom was then asked by classmates to guess what the other student was miming (i.e., *Qu'est-ce qu'il faisait quand tu as frappé à la porte?*), thus creating an obligatory context for use of the *imparfait* (e.g., *were you brushing your teeth?* etc.).

The thematic context of the treatment materials highlighting the hypothetical meaning of the conditional in Day and Shapson's (1991) classroom study involved the planning of an imaginary space colony. The context was presented to students first via a headline appearing in a newspaper from the future: "The problem of over-population is getting worse! Some courageous pioneers are going to have to leave to establish a colony in space." Students were asked to play the role of ecologists invited by CANADESPACE to design a space station that would recreate a natural environment where 1000 space pioneers would be able to settle. This provided students with contexts for using the conditional to express possible yet uncertain outcomes in the future. In groups of four, students had to make a model of their plan and then present an oral report to the class to describe and justify their plan. They then had to prepare a written report describing each part of the colony and its importance, as well as a newspaper article describing what life would be like for the space pioneers. Another important feature of the unit was that every lesson began with a language game or exercise that served to reinforce the functions of the conditional. In one game, to practice using (and not using) conditionals as politeness markers, students created then role-played situations in which requests were made first by an "authoritarian" person then by a courteous person. In another game, the teacher gave competing teams 10 minutes to generate as many hypothetical outcomes as possible to complete a set of clauses expressing a condition of the type "If I had a million dollars. . . .." The teacher then chose one of the clauses at random and asked teams to complete it in as many ways as possible in 30 seconds. In yet another game, students had to choose the correct hypothetical outcome in a series of experiments, which they could feasibly try out at home, and then discuss reasons for their choice. A game also provided important production practice in Wright's (1996) instructional unit on verbs of motion. After students played the roles of predators and prey during physical education activities, discussion of their strategies for survival elicited the productive use of target verbs.

In Lyster's (1994a) study of the effects of instruction on immersion students' use of second-person pronouns, practice activities were implemented that required students to give directions using appropriate pronouns in various role plays. In a whole-class activity, the teacher assigned formal roles to various students who in turn had to ask individual students for directions in or around the school. The teacher began the lesson by assigning the role of President of the Parent-Teacher Association to a student who then asked a classmate, "Pouvez-vous m'indiquer où est le gymnase?" In his reply, the respondent consistently confounded *tu* and *vous* forms, but prompted by students' comments and supportive laughter, he self-corrected. He concluded his lengthy explanation (the gymnasium happened to be quite far from the classroom) hesitatingly with ". . . *et tu es là . . . vous es là . . . vous êtes là!*" which earned him a round of applause from fellow students. The next student asked by the alleged PTA president to give directions succeeded in maintaining the use of *vous* throughout, a feat that also culminated in applause from classmates. The activity proceeded as such with a considerable amount of teacher correction as well as peer correction. Students then played a game in pairs using a map of Quebec City in which they exchanged status roles in a range of formal and informal settings (e.g., "You're coming out of the Couvent des Ursulines, rue du Parloir, and an elderly lady whom you don't know asks you how to get to the Manège Militaire;" "You're walking along the Dufferin Terrace and a boy your age asks you how to get to Dufferin Avenue"). Each student began with five tokens, and had to give to his or her partner directions appropriate to the context. If a student used *tu* in a formal context or *vous* in an informal context, and his or her partner caught the error, the student had to concede a token.

In Harley's (1998) gender study with Grade 2 children, many of the opportunities for production practice occurred during songs, riddles, and games. To play 'My Aunt's Suitcase' each student in turn added an item to a memorized list of things packed in the aunt's suitcase; items could be all masculine, all feminine, or all with a certain ending. To win at 'Bingo' students had to name the objects, using correct gender, in the winning row or column they had filled. In a board game called 'The Race', a student landing on a square had to choose a picture card and name the object along with the correct gender-specific article. For production practice in Lyster's (2004a) gender study with Grade 5 students, teachers were provided with scores of riddles on flash cards, eliciting target words either from the students' curriculum or other high-frequency lexical items, to use at any time throughout the treatment as a whole-class or small-group activity. For example, the riddle "*I divide the property of two neighbours. What am I?*" elicited the response "*une clôture*" (a fence), which needed to include the correct determiner in order to be accepted. In addition, after exposure to various rhymes and songs, students were asked to create their own rhyming verses. The most consistent opportunities for production practice in Lyster's study were created by specific types of feedback, a strategy further elaborated in Chapter 4. Given the generally rich context for language use in content-based classrooms, strategic feedback may prove to be the most efficient way of pushing learners in their output during meaning-focused interaction. As Lightbown (1998) argued, "Work on improving output is better done in the context of more interactive activities, in which the main focus is on communication, but in which the accuracy or sophistication can be improved via focus on form via feedback and learners' self-corrections" (p. 194).

4. Summary

This chapter considered a range of instructional activities that enable students to process language through content in ways that have variable effects on target language learning. Instructional techniques used by teachers to make subject matter comprehensible for students are at the core of content-based approaches, but the kinds of paralinguistic and also verbal support that teachers provide to facilitate comprehension need to be counterbalanced with efforts to increasingly ensure that the demands placed on learners are cognitively engaging. A content-based approach with extensive exposure to comprehensible input ensures a great deal of target language learning, especially high-frequency and phonologically salient items, but needs to be complemented by proactive form-focused instruction targeting less salient target features. Moreover, typical content-based tasks requiring oral interaction tend to be cognitively demanding and context-embedded, and so need to be complemented by written tasks that are context-reduced in a way that pushes learners away from their reliance on paralinguistic support for task completion. To ensure that students are pushed to use specific target forms that are otherwise avoided or misused in oral production, typical content-based tasks need to be counterbalanced with proactive form-focused instruction. In this chapter, a proactive approach to form-focused instruction was operationalized as a balanced distribution of activities interweaving opportunities for noticing, awareness, and practice.

Noticing activities serve as effective catalysts for drawing learners' attention to problematic target features that have been contrived to appear more salient and/or frequent in oral and written input (for example, by means of typographical enhancement). Their aim is to initiate the process of analysis and to effect change towards more target-like representations of the target language. Awareness activities, which include inductive rule-discovery tasks and opportunities to compare and contrast language patterns, followed by different types of metalinguistic information, generally serve to consolidate the restructuring of rule-based declarative representations. As learners engage in production practice ranging from communicative practice to controlled practice, they are given important opportunities to proceduralise their newly analyzed knowledge of emerging forms. Production practice entails cognitively undemanding tasks that range from communicative practice at the context-embedded end of the continuum of contextual support (e.g., designing futuristic space colonies or creating childhood albums) to controlled practice at the context-reduced end of the continuum (e.g., language games, role plays, riddles). The next chapter moves away from pre-planned proactive interventions and considers reactive form-focused instruction, designed to engage learners with language in the context of teacher-student interaction.

CHAPTER 4

Negotiating language through content

The preceding chapter considered proactive form-focused instruction, addressing both receptive and production practice activities, including collaborative tasks designed to provide students with opportunities to interact with one another. This chapter now considers reactive form-focused instruction and the central role played by teachers as they interact with students during whole-class activities with the dual aim of enhancing their students' content knowledge and language development. The intention is not to eschew peer interaction but rather to acknowledge the importance of teacher-student interaction in settings where class time devoted to whole-class activities usually exceeds time devoted to group activities. This chapter addresses the need to counterbalance diverse opportunities to negotiate language through content during teacher-student interaction by means of instructional options that vary from scaffolding to corrective feedback.

1. Whole-class interaction

In schools, teacher-led lessons involving whole-class interaction tend to occupy a greater portion of time than do dyadic or group activities involving peer interaction. For example, in their analysis of videotaped mathematics lessons taught in 231 Grade 8 classrooms across the US, Germany, and Japan, Stigler and Hiebert (1999) found that the portion of time devoted to whole-class interaction was 70% in Germany and 60% in the US and Japan. Also in a non-immersion setting, Fazio and Lyster (1998) reported that 81% of class time in French mother-tongue language arts lessons was devoted to whole-class activities and 19% to individual seatwork; no observations of any group work were recorded. In CLIL classrooms in Austrian secondary schools, Dalton-Puffer (2006) reported a preponderance of teacher-led whole-class activities interspersed occasionally with student presentations and group-work activities. In immersion settings, Lyster and Mori (2006) reported that 57% of class time in Japanese immersion classrooms and 70% of class time in French immersion classrooms was devoted to whole-class activities, while only 14% of class time was devoted to group work in both French and Japanese immersion classrooms. Two of the immersion teachers interviewed by Salomone (1992a) estimated that 75–80% of the time in kindergarten and 65% in Grade 2 was devoted to whole-class activities. She found that immersion classrooms were "usually limited to teacher-fronted activities for several reasons: the teacher's need for classroom control, lack of student second language ability, and the need for second language input from the only native speaker in the classroom" (p. 29). Results of Netten's (1991) observational study of immersion classrooms, however, call into question the importance typically attributed to immersion 'teacher-talk' and revealed instead that interaction between teacher and students and also among students "may permit more experimentation with the language, leading to higher levels of competence in the second language" (p. 303). Similarly, Haneda (2005) remarked that whole-class interaction is "a major site for second language learning and teaching in the everyday reality of classrooms" (p. 314).

Teacher-fronted lessons can be used effectively in combination with group and pair work in complementary ways, as observed by Gibbons (2003) during science lessons in content-based ESL classrooms. Some lessons consisted entirely of students carrying out experiments in small groups, while in other lessons the teacher played a major role in initiating talk: "Observing one or another of these lessons might lead to a conclusion that the classroom was teacher fronted and teacher directed or, conversely, that it was totally student centered" (p. 255). Gibbons' observational study helps to "shift pedagogical questions away from the well-worn debate around traditional/teacher-fronted versus progressive/student-centred pedagogies toward a focus on the nature of the discourse itself and its mediating role in the broader knowledge framework of the curriculum" (Gibbons 2003: 268). In other words, more important than whether the lesson is a whole-class or small-group activity is the quality of the interaction and the extent to which it contributes to educational objectives. This chapter explores how teachers in immersion and content-based classrooms can enhance the quality of their interactions with students to ensure that learning, in addition to communication, is taking place. The concern in this chapter is with teacher-student interaction that emphasizes the active role played by both teacher and students as full-fledged participants in classroom discourse.

2.   IRF exchanges and teacher questions

In their seminal study of classroom discourse, Sinclair and Coulthard (1975) found that the most typical teaching exchange consists of three moves: an initiating (I) move by the teacher (e.g., elicitation, directive, question); a responding (R) move by the student (e.g., reply, acknowledgement); and a follow-up (F) move by the teacher (e.g., evaluation, acceptance). The so-called IRF sequence is also known as the initiation-response-evaluation (IRE) sequence or 'triadic dialogue' (Lemke 1990). The IRF sequence is seen as the quintessence of transmission models of teaching and typical of teacher-centred classrooms. It has been criticized for engaging students only minimally and for maintaining unequal power relationships between teachers and students. Nevertheless, the IRF sequence continues to permeate classroom discourse and has been regaining its credibility as an important pedagogical tool in constructivist approaches to education.

Mercer (1999) suggested that teachers' reliance on IRF sequences and frequent questions serve to monitor students' knowledge and understanding. That is, by assessing their students in an ongoing manner in the course of interaction, teachers are better equipped to plan and evaluate their teaching. Similarly, Nassaji and Wells (2000) remarked that, in classroom discourse, "it is necessary for somebody to ensure that the discussion proceeds in an orderly manner and that, as far as possible, all participants contribute to, and benefit from the co-construction of knowledge" (p. 378). In their analysis of literature and science classes from Grades 1 to 6, they found a prevalence of IRF exchanges, even among teachers who were attempting to create a more dialogic style of interaction. They found that IRF exchanges played an important role in initiating discussion and that the teacher's opening move enabled both students and teachers alike to contribute substantively to understanding an issue for which there was no single correct answer and in which the goal was to consider a variety of alternatives. That the exchange frequently began with a question, they argued, "is hardly surprising, since a question both proposes an issue for discussion and, because of its high level of prospectiveness, requires the recipient(s) to contribute to the issue in response" (Nassaji & Wells 2000:400).

Teachers' initiating moves in the IRF exchange are usually epistemic questions considered to be either display questions (to which the teacher knows the answer) or referential questions (to which the teacher does not know the answer). Referential questions can be either open (with many possible answers) or closed (with only one possible answer). Display questions are generally thought to limit the students' possibilities to try out their own ideas, but teachers have been observed using both display and referential questions with equal effectiveness (Haneda 2005). In immersion classrooms, Salomone (1992b) remarked that display questions "are an important part of content learning" (p. 104), because they help teachers to verify content mastery and thus are not limited to inciting students only to display linguistic knowledge. Similarly, in Italian content-based classes, Musumeci (1996) found that display questions served effectively to verify comprehension of subject matter delivered in the second language and were just as effective as referential questions for eliciting extensive responses from students. Based on analyses of instructional discourse in CLIL classrooms, Dalton-Puffer (2006) argued against adopting "an over-simple understanding of classroom language being divided between 'natural, authentic and open-ended' referential questions on the one hand, and 'unnatural, artificial and closed' display questions on the other" (p. 205).

As exemplary instructional practice in second language classrooms, Long (2007: 115) called for fewer display questions and more referential questions, along with recasts (see next section), and, by way of example, provided the following exchange initiated by a teacher's referential question:

> T: *What's the meaning of that tattoo?*
> S: *It mean a fan this band.*
> T: *It means you're a Chumbawumba fan? My goodness! A really serious fan!*

While the content of this exchange is doubtlessly effective at lowering students' affective filter in important ways, it falls short of instantiating a model exchange, rich in discourse and with significant educational purpose, whereby opportunities are maximized for both language development and content learning. It may be the case that criticisms of the overuse of display questions apply to traditional language classrooms more than to content-based classrooms (but see McCormick & Donato 2000). In content-based classrooms, notwithstanding a constructivist rationale for co-constructing knowledge and negotiating content, it appears both improbable and undesirable for subject-matter specialists to ask a preponderance of questions to which they do not know the answers. As they work dialogically with students, teachers need to exercise their responsibility as mentors interacting with novices by providing scaffolding that necessitates a variety of questioning techniques ranging from display to referential questions.

Arguably more important than the teacher's initial question in the IRF exchange is the teacher's choice of follow-up move and the extent to which it allows the teacher to work with the student's response in a variety of ways.

Nassaji and Wells (2000) found that IRF exchanges beginning with a display question "can develop into more equal dialogue if, in the follow-up move, the teacher avoids evaluation and instead requests justifications, connections or counter-arguments and allows students to self-select in making their contributions" (pp. 400–401). Haneda (2005) also argued that teacher follow-up moves should not be restricted to evaluative comments and instead should aim to: (a) elaborate on the student's response or provide clarification; (b) request further elaboration, justification, explanation, or exemplification; (c) challenge students' views. Drawing on the work of Collins (1982) and the premise that "the quality of conversational exchanges between teachers and students influences student achievement" (Collins 1982:430), Haneda (2005) pointed to the important role played by follow-up moves that incorporate student responses into subsequent teacher questions.

Similarly, Echarvarria and Graves (1998) drew on Tharpe and Gallimore's (1988:134) proposal for "instructional conversations," a reactive approach used with small groups of children to provide assistance and instruction that are contingent on student production. Specifically in the context of content-based instruction, Echarvarria and Graves (1998) classified three types of helpful questioning techniques designed to enrich instructional conversations and to facilitate students' understanding of ideas and concepts that they would otherwise be unable to express on their own:

1. Promotion of more complex language and expression
   a. "Tell me more about..."
   b. "What do you mean by..."
   c. "In other words..."
   d. "Why do you think that?"

2. Elicitation of bases for statements or positions
   a. "How do you know?"
   b. "What makes you think that?"

3. Fewer known-answer questions
   a. "Look at the page and tell me what you think the chapter will be about."
   b. "What can you learn from reading this label?"
   c. "How are these plants different?"
   d. "Why would the colonists do that?"
   e. "Tell me more about that."
   f. "On what basis would you group these objects?"
   g. "Why might that be?"
   h. "What makes you think this might be different?"

Similarly, to create more opportunities for extended student responses specifically in CLIL classrooms, Dalton-Puffer (2006) recommended that teachers could use fewer questions eliciting facts, which tend to result in minimal responses, and more questions about students' beliefs and opinions that require them to explain, define, or give reasons.

3.   Negotiated scaffolding and feedback

In addition to various questioning techniques, teacher follow-up moves include feedback. Many research studies conducted in immersion classrooms have suggested, however, that the use of feedback is not high on teachers' list of priorities. The observation study of immersion classrooms described by Allen et al. (1990) revealed that error treatment was dealt with in "a confusing and unsystematic way" (p. 67) and that "teachers spent only minimal amounts of observed time asking students what they intended in producing a specific utterance or written text" (p. 77). They cautioned that such "unsystematic, possibly random feedback to learners about their language errors" (p. 76) could have a "detrimental effect on learning" (p. 67). Day and Shapson (1996), in their observations of immersion classrooms, also found error feedback to be infrequent. The French immersion teachers observed by Chaudron (1977, 1986) provided feedback, but did so more during language arts classes than subject-matter lessons and earlier in the school year than later. Salomone (1992a) found that errors were of little consequence to immersion teachers: "They were corrected simply by teachers' modelling of the correction" (pp. 24–35). Salomone (1992b: 100) explained that "the immersion philosophy is not to correct errors but rather to model the correct response for the learners, as suggested in the Immersion Teacher Handbook (Snow 1987: 22)." Netten (1991) also found that immersion teachers encouraged communication by correcting oral errors "as unobtrusively as possible, usually by echoing the pupil's response" (p. 299). It seems highly probable that a correlation exists between immersion teachers' tendency to use random implicit feedback and immersion students' tendency to reach a developmental plateau in their communicative ability.

The observation that immersion teachers provide feedback only minimally may be the result of a well-known paradox, summarized by Chaudron (1988: 134) as follows: "teachers must either interrupt communication for the sake of formal correction or let errors pass 'untreated' in order to further the communicative goals of classroom interaction." However, this may be a false paradox. Plenty of classroom studies have shown that teachers are able to provide various forms of corrective feedback in ways that allow the communicative flow to continue. That teachers are able to provide feedback without inhibiting students and without interrupting conversational coherence supports the argument that students not only expect corrective feedback as an integral part of classroom discourse (Lyster & Ranta 1997; De Pietro, Matthey, & Py 1989; van Lier 1988) but also prefer receiving feedback over having their errors ignored (e.g., Cathcart & Olsen 1977; Oladejo 1993; Schulz 1996, 2001). Teachers, therefore, do not have to choose between communication on the one hand and corrective feedback on the other, because both can be effectively integrated in instructional discourse (e.g., Ammar & Spada 2006; Doughty & Varela 1998; Ellis, Basturkmen, & Loewen 2001; Lyster 2004a; Spada & Lightbown 1993). In fact, recent studies of immersion classrooms have shown that immersion teachers provide feedback after an average of 67% of their students' errors in French immersion classrooms (Lyster & Ranta 1997), 61% in Japanese immersion classrooms (Lyster & Mori 2006), and 64% in English immersion classrooms (Lee 2006). In all cases, the majority of the feedback used by immersion teachers involves recasting.

3.1 Recasting

One of the most frequent types of feedback observed in a range of second language classroom settings is the recast, defined as a reformulation of the learner's utterance minus the error(s). Recasts are by far the most frequently used feedback across a spectrum of classroom settings: elementary immersion classrooms in Canada (Lyster & Ranta 1997), the US (Mori 2002), and Korea (Lee 2006); university-level foreign language classrooms in Australia (Doughty 1994) and the US (Roberts 1995); high school EFL classrooms in Hong Kong (Tsang 2004) and a range of EFL instructional settings in Austria (Havranek 2002); adult ESL classrooms in New Zealand (Ellis et al. 2001) and Canada (Panova & Lyster 2002). Based on claims that children frequently repeat parental recasts during first language acquisition, recasts have been upheld as a type of feedback of prime importance, hypothesized to create ideal opportunities for learners to notice the difference between their interlanguage forms and target-like reformulations (e.g., Doughty 2001; Long 1996, 2007). In the context of content-based and immersion classrooms, however, research suggests instead that the strength of recasts may lie more in their propensity for facilitating the delivery of complex subject matter and for providing helpful scaffolding to learners when target forms are beyond their current abilities (Gibbons 1998, 2003; Lyster 1998a, 2002a; Mohan & Beckett 2001).

In a mainstream primary classroom, Gibbons (1998, 2003) examined the development of academic discourse by 9–10-year-old learners of English. She described an instructional sequence about the topic of magnetism in the science class, consisting of small-group work, teacher-guided reporting, and journal writing. In the teacher-guided reporting stage, the teacher's aim was to extend the children's linguistic resources in a context-reduced situation and to focus on the specific discourse of science. To push students to use a more scientific register, the teacher used explicit comments such as: "We're trying to talk like scientists," "Your language has got to be really precise," and "The language you choose is very important" (Gibbons 1998:105). The teacher interacted with individual students in ways that scaffolded their contributions, "allowing for communication to proceed while giving the learner access to new linguistic data" (Gibbons 1998:110). Gibbons (2003) identified three main techniques that the teacher used during the stage of teacher-guided reporting to help the children reconstruct their experiences and develop shared understandings through language: (a) recasting, (b) signaling how to reformulate, and (c) indicating a need for reformulation. Defined as "any piece of connected discourse where a teacher rewords student meaning in more registrally appropriate ways" (Gibbons 2003:258), recasting was used by the teacher primarily to promote a shift towards a more scientific register, as in the following example:

> T: OK can you then tell me what you had to do next?
> S: when we had em the things the first one like if you put it up in the air like that . the magnets you can feel . feel the em . that they're not pushing?
> T: when you turn the magnet around? you felt that
> S: pushing and if we use the other side we can't feel pushing
> T: OK so when .. they were facing one way .. they/ you felt the magnets _attract_ and _stick together_/ when you turn one of the magnets around you felt it . _repelling_ .. or _pushing away_ .. OK thank you well done Charbel

In this example, the teacher reformulates the student's use of 'pushing' and 'not pushing' into the stylistically more appropriate forms that are at the heart of this lesson on magnetism: 'attract' and 'repel'. Gibbons (2003) invested such recasts with a style-shifting function and described their use as "an ongoing process of recapping by the teacher, who re-represents or recontextualizes learners' experiences and the events they are talking about in a way that fits the broader pedagogic objectives of the curriculum" (p. 257). The ways in which this same teacher signaled to her students the need to reformulate on their own are presented later in this chapter.

Mohan and Beckett (2001) argued that recasts are more effective for "editing discourse" than for correcting grammar and that, as shown in the following example, recasts serve as semantic paraphrases that help to maintain and develop academic discourse in content-based instructional contexts.

> S: To stop the brain's aging, *we can use our bodies and heads...*
> T: So, we can prevent our brain from getting weak *by being mentally and physically active?*

Mohan and Beckett provided several such examples of adult ESL learners engaged in a "zone of negotiation" with their teacher, who consistently provided recasts, not to correct grammar, but rather to provide models of more academically appropriate language. In a similar vein, Day and Shapson (1996:50) observed a Grade 7 immersion teacher who frequently paraphrased what students said, often in the form of recast, as in the following example:

> S: *Qu'est-ce qui fait le travail du membrane?*
>   [What does the work of the membrane?]
> T: *Qu'est-ce que le membrane fait dans son travail?*
>   [What does the membrane do in its work?]

Assuming that this technique was a form of corrective feedback provided during content instruction, the researchers asked the teacher what her objective was. Her response suggested that formal correction was not her primary purpose. More in line with Mohan and Beckett's (2001) view of recasts as semantic paraphrases serving as models of more academically appropriate language, she used paraphrasing "to provide students with a mirror they could use in checking their thoughts ... and at the same time to promote a general learning strategy or tool that could be used in understanding French" (Day & Shapson 1996:50).

Classroom observational studies have identified recasts as the most frequent type of feedback used by immersion teachers, accounting for 55% of all feedback provided in French immersion classrooms in Canada (Lyster & Ranta 1997), 65% in Japanese immersion classrooms in the US (Lyster & Mori 2006), and 53% in English immersion classrooms in Korea (Lee 2006). That immersion teachers across these instructional settings use recasts much more frequently than other types of feedback can be seen as well tuned to the objectives of content-based second language instruction. That is, recasts serve to maintain the flow of communication, to keep students' attention focused on content, and to provide scaffolds that enable learners to participate in interaction about subject matter that requires linguistic abilities exceeding their current developmental level. In addition, recasts serve as exemplars of positive evidence that can be expected to facilitate the encoding of new target representations (Braidi 2002; Leeman 2003), but only in discourse contexts where they cannot be perceived ambiguously as approving the use of non-target forms.

Lyster (1998a) argued that many recasts are sources of linguistic ambiguity, which may even contribute to immersion students' continued use of non-target forms. The ambiguity in content-based classrooms derives in part from the ubiquitous appearance of recasts in confirmations, confirmation checks, or expansions, all intended to confirm or disconfirm the veracity of the student's message. These very same discourse functions motivate the even more ubiquitous use of non-corrective repetition by content-based teachers, an example of which follows:

> T: *Ça c'est à-peu-près quelle grandeur, mes amis?*
>   [That's about what size, my friends?]
> S: *La grandeur de ta règle.* [The size of your ruler.]
> T: *La grandeur de ta règle? Excellent, à-peu- près.*
>   [The size of your ruler? Excellent, just about.]

Lyster (1998a) found that non-corrective repetition occurred even more frequently than recasts in French immersion classrooms and that, together, recasts and non-corrective repetition followed almost one-third of all student utterances. Recasts and non-corrective repetition were both used to provide or seek confirmation or additional information related to the student's message. Whether immersion teachers recast ill-formed utterances or repeated well-formed utterances, their intentions appeared to coincide with one or more of the following functions attributed to repetition in classroom discourse by Weiner and Goodenough (1977): (a) to acknowledge the content of the student's utterance; (b) to "rebroadcast" the student's message in order to ensure that the whole class has heard; and (c) to hold the floor and thereby buy time to plan the next move. Carpenter, Jeon, MacGregor, and Mackey (2006) found that even adult learners, as they viewed video-taped segments of a researcher responding to a learner with a mixture of recasts and non-corrective repetition, were more likely to identify recasts as non-corrective repetition than as recasts – regardless of whether or not they actually heard the learner's preceding utterance. Similarly, Braidi (2002) concluded that, in a laboratory setting, it was impossible to determine whether learner responses to recasts addressed form or meaning, as in: "Yes, I recognize that that is the correct form" versus "Yes, that is what I meant to say" (p. 31; see also Lyster 1998a). Take for instance the following exchange between a learner of English and a native speaker, recorded in a laboratory setting by Mackey, Gass, and McDonough (2000: 486):

> L: *It have mixed colors.*
> NS: *It has mixed colors.*
> L: *Mixed colors, aha.*

In a stimulated-recall session during which the learner was asked to comment while reviewing a video recording of the exchange, the learner reported, "I was thinking ... nothing, she just repeat what I said," thus revealing that this learner perceived no difference between the target form 'It has' and the non-target form 'It have'. If recasts such as these can be perceived as non-corrective repetition in dyadic interaction in laboratory settings, what are the odds that the modification might be perceived by learners engaged in the hurly-burly interaction of classrooms, especially those that are content-based and otherwise communicatively oriented?

Teachers have been observed amplifying the ambiguity of recasts by frequently using signs of approval as positive feedback – including affirmations such as *oui*, *c'est ça*, and *OK*, and praise markers such as *Très bien*, *Bravo*, and *Excellent*. Lyster (1998a) found that teachers used signs of approval equally often with recasts, non-corrective repetition, and even topic-continuation moves immediately following errors. The indiscriminate use of signs of approval with both recasts and non-corrective repetition alike suggests further that teachers use recasts and non-corrective repetition to fulfil similar discourse functions (i.e., to confirm or disconfirm the veracity of learners' messages) and do not consistently use recasts to provide negative evidence (i.e., information about ungrammaticality). In addition to the teacher's own intent, whether or not a learner perceives the corrective function of a recast depends on many other factors:

– Recasts are more likely to be noticed by high-ability learners than by low-ability learners (Ammar & Spada 2006; Lin & Hedgcock 1996; Mackey & Philp 1998; Netten 1991).

– Recasts of phonological errors are more noticeable than recasts of grammatical errors (Carpenter et al. 2006; Lyster 1998b; Mackey, Gass, & McDonough 2000).

– Recasts that reduce the learner's initial utterance then add intonational stress for emphasis are more likely to draw attention to the mismatch than

recasts that are neither reduced nor stressed (Ellis & Sheen 2006; Loewen & Philp 2006; Nicholas, Lightbown, & Spada 2001).
– Recasts in laboratory settings are effective when they are provided intensively and with consistency to developmentally ready learners receiving individualized attention (Han 2002).
– Recasts may benefit language development when "the learner has already begun to use a particular linguistic feature and is in a position to choose between linguistic alternatives" (Nicholas et al. 2001:752; see also Han 2002).

Because recasts preserve the learners' intended meaning, Long (1996) argued that recasts free up cognitive resources that would otherwise be used for semantic processing. Thus, with meaning held constant, recasts have the potential to enable learners to focus on form and to notice errors in their interlanguage production (see also Doughty 2001). Lyster and Mori (in press) argued, however, that this is only likely to be the case in form-oriented classrooms (see also Nicholas et al. 2001) where the emphasis on accuracy primes learners to notice the corrective function of recasts. Ellis and Sheen (2006) made a similar argument:

> It is not possible to say with any certainty whether recasts constitute a source of negative evidence (as it is often assumed) or afford only positive evidence, as this will depend on the learner's orientation to the interaction. If learners treat language as an object to be studied, then they may detect the corrective force of recasts and thus derive negative evidence from them. But if they act as language users and treat language as a tool, then they are less likely to see recasts as corrective and so will derive only positive evidence from them.
>
> (pp. 596–597)

Recasts have even proven to be as salient as explicit correction in foreign language settings, including traditional classrooms in which German is taught as a foreign language in Belgium (Lochtman 2002) and Japanese immersion classrooms in the US (Lyster & Mori 2006). In meaning-oriented second language classrooms, however, when students' attention is focused on meaning via recasting, they remain focused on meaning, not form, because they expect the teacher's immediate response to confirm or disconfirm the veracity of their utterances (Lyster 2002a).

Long (2007) argued that recasts provide teachers in immersion and other content-based classrooms with "the option of dealing with many of their students' language problems *incidentally* while working on their subject matter of choice" (pp. 76–77). This recommendation, however, overlooks a considerable amount of research documenting that an incidental approach to language teaching and learning has indeed been widely adopted in immersion and content-based settings (and has been since their inception), including extensive recasting, but with disappointing effects on students' interlanguage development (see Chapter 2 and also Day & Shapson 1996; Netten 1991; Lyster & Mori 2006; Lyster & Ranta 1997; Salomone 1992a). A number of studies conducted in both laboratory and classroom settings and synthesized in overviews by DeKeyser (2003), Norris and Ortega (2001), and Spada (1997) reveal that instructional treatments involving explicit learning (i.e., awareness of what is being learned) are more effective than implicit treatments. Spada (1997) found that drawing attention to form explicitly was more effective than implicit attempts especially in communicative and content-based classroom settings. As outlined throughout this book, there is considerable consensus among researchers familiar with immersion and content-based classrooms that a more systematic and less incidental approach to language pedagogy needs to be integrated into the curriculum because there now exists considerable evidence that a prevalence of implicit and incidental treatment of language in these particular instructional settings does not enable students to engage with language in ways that ensure their continued language growth.

A closer look at interaction in a Grade 4 science lesson observed by Lyster (1998d, 2002b) illustrates the ambiguity of recasts from a learner's perspective and their lack of salience in content-based lessons. The science lesson is about the water cycle and is taught by Marie to her Grade 4 middle-immersion students. Along with many signs of approval to encourage her students, Marie uses both recasts and non-corrective repetitions alike to confirm and disconfirm what students say and to provide scaffolding that enables them to express meanings that they would be unable to convey on their own.

1) T: *Qu'est-ce que c'est un ruisseau encore? ... Oui?*	1) T: *What's a stream again? ... Yes?*
2) S1: *C'est comme un petit lac.*	2) S1: *It's like a small lake.*
3) T: *Un petit lac qu'on a dit?*	3) T: *Did we say a small lake?*
4) S2: *C'est un petit rivière.*	4) S2: *It's a small [wrong gender] river.*
5) T: *C'est ça. C'est plus une petite rivière, OK? Parce qu'un lac c'est comme un endroit où il y a de l'eau mais c'est un. . . ?*	5) T: *That's it. It's more like a little river, OK? Because a lake it's like a place where there's water but it's a. . . ?*
6) Ss: *Comme un cercle.*	6) Ss: *Like a circle.*

7) T: C'est comme un cercle [. . .].
Puis là elle se retrouve près
d'une forêt. Et qu'est-ce qu'ils
font dans la forêt? William?

8) S3:   Ils coupent des arbres.

9) T: Ils coupent des arbres. Et
quand on coupe des arbres et
qu'on est en plein milieu de
la forêt, est-ce qu'on peut
amener un camion puis
mettre le bois dedans? . . .
Qu'est-ce qu'on fait pour
transporter le bois?

10) S4:   Euh, tu mets le bois dans
l'eau et les euh, comment
dis-tu euh [carries]?

11) Ss: Emporte.

12) T: Emporte, bien.

13) S4:   Emporte le arbre au un place
puis un autre personne qui
met le bois.

14) T: C'est ça. Alors, on met le bois
dans la rivière pour qu'il soit
transporté d'un endroit à
l'autre.

7) T: It's like a circle [. . .]. And
then she finds herself near a
forest. And what is it that
they do in the forest?
William?

8) S3:   They cut down trees.

9) T: They cut down trees. And
when you cut down trees and
you're right in the middle of
the forest, can you bring a
truck and then put the wood
in it? . . . What do they do to
transport the wood?

10) S4:   Um, you put the wood in the
water and the um, how do
you say um /carries/?

11) Ss: 'Emporte'.

12) T: Emporte, good.

13) S4:   Carries tree to an place and
another person who puts the
wood.

14) T: That's it. So, they put the
wood in the river so it gets
transported from one place to
another.

Marie begins by asking students to define *un ruisseau* ("a stream"). In a confirmation check in turn 3, she repeats a student's response (*un petit lac* "a small lake") to disconfirm this incorrect yet well-formed response. The next student's answer (*un petit rivière* "a small river") is correct in terms of content although the grammatical gender is incorrect. Marie approves the content with *c'est ça* ("that's it") and then unobtrusively modifies the gender in her recast. In turn 7, she repeats the students' correct response *comme un cercle* ("like a circle") and then in turn 9 repeats verbatim William's response, *ils coupent des arbres* ("they cut trees"), each of which is accurate in both form and meaning. Next is a good example of collective scaffolding as a student in turn 10 tries to describe how the wood is transported, but needs to ask how to say "carries" in French. His classmates respond in turn 11 with *emporte*, which enables him to continue in turn 13 with *Emporte le arbre au un place puis un autre personne qui met le bois* ("Carries tree to an place and another person who puts the wood"), an ill-formed utterance met with Marie's approval in turn 14 (*C'est ça* "that's it").

As the exchange continues, Marie draws her students attention to a lone water drop, brought to life as the young Perlette.

15) T:	*Au moment où il parle à Perlette, qu'est-ce qui arrive au beau poisson?*		15) T:	*While he's talking to Perlette, what happens to the handsome fish?*
16) S5:	*Il va la boire.*		16) S5:	*He's going to drink her.*
17) T:	*Il va la boire? Non, il va pas boire Perlette.*		17) T:	*He's going to drink her? No, he's not going to drink Perlette.*
18) S6:	*Euh, le poisson est une amie de elle.*		18) S6:	*Um, the fish is a friend of her.*
19) T:	*Oui, c'est ça, ce sont des amis puis ils parlent ensemble. Et tout à coup, qu'est-ce qui se passe? Oui?*		19) T:	*Yes, that's it, they're friends and they talk together. Then suddenly what happens? Yes?*
20) S7:	*Une personne qui pêche a pris.*		20) S7:	*A person who is fishing took.*
21) T:	*Exactement. Il arrive un hameçon avec un petit vers de terre dedans et là le poisson se retourne... et là il est pris avec son hameçon et il s'en va lui aussi.*		21) T:	*Exactly. A fishing hook shows up with a little worm on it and so the fish turns around... and then he gets stuck on the fishing hook and so away he goes too.*

When Marie asks what happens to the fish, a student in turn 16 replies that it intends to drink Perlette. Marie repeats this in her follow-up turn as a confirmation check because the student's well-formed statement (*Il va la boire* "He's going to drink her") is untrue. A true but ill-formed statement is then proposed in turn 18 (*le poisson est une ami de elle* "the fish is a friend of her"), which is met first with Marie's approval (*Oui, c'est ça* "Yes, that's it") then with a confirming recast (*ce sont des amis* "they're friends") before Marie continues with her questions about what happens next. The student's non-target utterance in turn 20 (*Une personne qui pêche a pris* "A person who is fishing took") is again followed by approval (*Exactement* "Exactly") and then an expansion of the student's message, but without any recast of specific forms.

The focus of the exchange then returns to the adventures of Perlette.

22) T: *Alors là, elle décide de demander au soleil de venir la réchauffer. Pourquoi pensez-vous qu'elle veut se faire réchauffer? Oui?*	22) T: *And then she decides to ask the sun to come and warm her up. Why do you think she wants to warm herself up? Yes?*
23) S8: *Parce qu'elle est trop froid pour aller dans toute les [?]*	23) S8: *Because she has too cold to go into all the [?]*
24) T: *Parce qu'elle a froid, OK. Oui?*	24) T: *Because she is cold, OK. Yes?*
25) S9: *Elle est trop peur.*	25) S9: *She has too frightened.*
26) T: *Parce qu'elle a peur, oui.*	26) T: *Because she is frightened, yes.*

Marie's question about Perlette in turn 22 elicits two student responses, both containing well-known errors made by second language learners of French in the use of auxiliary verbs. The first response in turn 23 (*parce qu'elle est trop froid* "because she has too cold") is followed by a recast in turn 24 (*parce qu'elle a froid* "because she is cold") as well as by the approval marker *OK*. The next non-target utterance in turn 25 (*elle est trop peur* "she is too frightened") is also followed by a recast in Marie's follow-up turn as well as by a sign of approval, *Oui*. The distinctions between various forms of *avoir* and *être*, in terms of both phonology and semantics, are a source of confusion for immersion students whose persistent misanalysis of these auxiliary and lexical verbs is apt to block entry into a major grammatical subsystem (Harley 1993). Arguably, recasts in response to errors caused by the wrong selection of one of two forms comprising a binary distinction (e.g., *be/have, être/avoir, his/her, le/la, a/the*) are inherently ambiguous, if there is nothing overtly disapproving in the recast, as they may appear to confirm that the two forms are interchangeable. Learners may not notice the subtle modification, but, even if they do, they could infer that the recast is an alternative way of saying the same thing (Lyster 1998a).

3.2 Negotiation for meaning

According to Long's (1996) revised interaction hypothesis, interaction plays a key role in driving second language development forward, because a primary source of positive and negative data (i.e., what is possible and not possible to say in the target language) is made available to learners during meaningful interaction with a more competent speaker. Interaction also provides learners with opportunities to control the input to some extent, as they ask their interlocutors to modify their speech in ways that make the input more accessible and more likely to be integrated into the learners' developing interlanguage system (Gass 1997; Long 1983, 1996; Pica 1994). In addition, interaction enables learners to test their hypotheses as it provides them with crucial information about their communicative success (Long 1977) along with important opportunities for modifying or reprocessing non-target output (e.g., Pica et al. 1989; Swain 1985, 1995).

In SLA research, conversational moves used in dyadic interaction to facilitate comprehension and hypothesized to benefit second language development are generally subsumed under the rubric of "negotiation for meaning." According to Long (1996), negotiation for meaning comprises the following types of interactional features:

– input modifications (e.g., stress on key words, decomposition, partial self-repetition)
– semantically contingent responses (e.g., recasts, repetition, expansions)
– conversational modifications (e.g., confirmations, confirmation checks, comprehension checks, clarification requests)

Long (1996) argued that these interactional features converge to provide learners with a primary source of negative evidence in ways that benefit second language development. The interaction hypothesis has generated a considerable amount of research, allowing researchers to investigate the nature and effects of interaction between learners and native speakers of the target language in laboratory settings, between learners and teachers in classroom settings, and between learners and other learners in either laboratory or classroom settings. Much research documenting the role of interaction has investigated dyads composed of a learner and a native speaker, examining various conversational moves used to solve problems in message comprehensibility, such as clarification requests, confirmation checks (including recasts and repetition), and comprehension checks (e.g., Brock, Crookes, Day, & Long 1986; Gass & Varonis 1994; Oliver 1995; Lin & Hedgcock 1996; Van den Branden 1997; Mackey & Philp 1998; Braidi 2002; Philp 2003). Findings have generally confirmed that these conversational moves provide learners and their interlocutors with useful strategies for facilitating comprehension (e.g., Pica, Young, & Doughty 1987). There is also evidence that, in the context of laboratory settings, intensive recasts provided consistently on target features are effective for second language development (e.g., Han 2002; Ishida 2004; Mackey & Philp 1998). In addition, SLA research investigating learners interacting in dyads with either another learner or a native speaker has demonstrated that, although learners are exposed to more target-like input during interaction with native speakers, they use more interactional moves that are hypothesized to facilitate second language development during interaction with another learner (e.g., Mackey, Oliver, & Leeman 2003; Pica, Lincoln-Porter, Paninos, & Linnell 1996; Sato & Lyster, in press; Shehadeh 1999, 2001, 2003; Varonis & Gass 1985). However, it has yet to be established empirically that the larger number of negotiation moves in learner-learner dyads actually contributes to their second language development more than does interaction with fewer negotiation moves (Aston 1986).

A major challenge in interaction research has been to isolate various interactional features in ways that demonstrate a direct impact on second language development (Braidi 1995; Carroll 1999; Skehan 1998). As Aston (1986) argued, "the criteria by which instances of discourse procedures are assigned to the various categories used by these studies do at times seem fuzzy" (p. 132). For example, Foster and Ohta (2005) demonstrated that comprehension checks do not necessarily signal a communication breakdown and can instead serve to express agreement or encouragement to continue. Moreover, there is considerable overlap in the component moves that serve to negotiate for meaning with the alleged purpose of avoiding communication breakdown. For example, Long's (1983, 1996) taxonomy identified as discrete moves both formally defined devices (repetitions, recasts, expansions) and functionally defined devices (confirmations, confirmation checks, comprehension checks, clarification requests), suggesting that recasts and repetitions are distinguishable from confirmations and confirmation checks. Yet recasts and repetitions are the forms that perform these confirming functions – discourse functions that remain indiscriminately constant across recasts and repetition with respect to message content. For example, in her lesson about the water cycle, Marie used recasts and repetitions as confirmations and confirmation checks that served (a) to confirm meaning but disconfirm form, (b) to confirm form but disconfirm meaning, or (c) to confirm both form and meaning:

a) Recasts such as *"une petite rivière"* and *"elle a peur"* served to confirm the veracity of student responses but to disconfirm their form.
b) Repetitions such as *"un petit lac"* and *"Il va la boire?"* served to disconfirm the veracity of students' responses but to confirm the form.
c) Repetitions such as *"comme un cercle"* and *"Ils coupent des arbres"* served to confirm both the form and veracity of student responses.

The subject matter in Marie's lesson about the water cycle was complex for Grade 4 middle immersion students. Because she was familiar with both the content and her students' communicative abilities, Marie was able to make rich interpretations of her students' contributions, which provided them with the scaffolding they needed for the lesson to move ahead. As a result of various recasts and repetitions, Marie was able to enhance the input in ways that made it comprehensible, but she did not deliberately draw attention to discrepancies between her recasts and the students' non-target output. To increase the likelihood that learners will notice the gap between recasts and non-target forms, Long (2007) recently advocated the use of "corrective" recasts and also "focused" recasts and even written recasts, yet argued that a recast is a recast only if it is implicit, incidental, and focused on meaning – that is, a confirmation check. Distinguishing recasts from confirmation checks thus remains problematic in research on negotiation for meaning.

Although negotiation for meaning has been advocated as a central feature of content-based instruction (e.g., Genesee 1987; Met 1994; Rebuffot 1993; Tardif 1991), its component moves, which have proven relevant in dyadic conversations, have not proven to be of equal relevance or importance in classroom settings, neither in student-student interaction (Aston 1986; Foster 1998; Foster & Ohta 2005) nor in teacher-student interaction (Lyster 2002a; Musumeci 1996). Whereas communication breakdowns and negotiation for meaning are hypothesized to be effective catalysts for second language development when they occur during conversations between a learner and a "more competent interlocutor" (Long 1996: 451), Foster and Ohta (2005: 424–425) found "scarcely any evidence at all" of learners negotiating for meaning to verify what their conversation was about, but instead found evidence of "learners supporting each other, frequently expressing interest in what their interlocutor is saying and giving encouragement to continue." Moreover, Musumeci (1996: 318) argued that "what learners will do in a small-group or one-to-one exchange with native speakers in the experimental setting may not generalize at all to the whole-class multiple-learners-one-teacher situation of the classroom" (see also Lyster 2002a). Teacher-student interaction has a clearly pedagogical focus relating not only to the exchange of comprehensible messages, but also to formal accuracy, academic achievement, and literacy development.

In post-secondary content-based classes of Italian as a foreign language, Musumeci (1996) reported that teachers viewed negotiation for meaning less as a language teaching strategy and more as a social strategy "to help the student get through the exchange as painlessly as possible" (p. 316). Whereas negotiation for meaning can facilitate comprehension, it also enables interlocutors to maintain rapport and display mutual satisfaction with the interaction, irrespective of their communicative success and mutual comprehension (Aston

1986). Musumeci (1996) found that teachers "appear to understand absolutely everything the students say" (p. 314). They strove to derive meaning from students' speech and, to do so, "supplied key lexical items and provided rich interpretations of student responses, rather than engage in the kind of negotiation which would have required learners to modify their own output" (p. 314). Musumeci further argued, "While this kind of 'filling in the spaces' by the teacher may have helped to create coherent conversational texts, it also made the teachers responsible for carrying the linguistic burden of the exchange, and it reduced the students' role to one of supplying linguistic 'hints' to the teacher, rather than functioning as full partners in the exchange" (p. 315). Her observation is thus reminiscent of Harley's (1993) conclusion regarding immersion classrooms with younger learners:

> A substantial portion of the effort in the communicative enterprise may be offloaded onto the teacher. This is doubtlessly appropriate and necessary in the early stages but in the long run may not encourage an independent approach to SLA that is seen as a prerequisite for expertise in any domain.   (p. 315)

Important to note nevertheless is Rodgers' (2006) recent finding that postsecondary students in three content-based Italian classes similar to those observed by Musumeci did make significant progress throughout the term in both content knowledge (i.e., Italian geography) and linguistic abilities, although he concluded that "there is still room to incorporate into this and other CBI [content-based instruction] contexts more opportunities for focusing on form" (p. 385).

As the name suggests, negotiation for meaning aims primarily to achieve "comprehensibility of message meaning" (Pica 1994: 494). Yet teachers and students are able to negotiate meaning with only minimal linguistic knowledge in common, by drawing on higher-order processes involving background and situational knowledge (Kleifgen & Saville-Troike 1992; Swain 1985). Moreover, experienced immersion teachers with daily exposure to their students' shared interlanguage become experts at understanding the interlanguage code (Lyster 2002a). Once students have acquired a language repertoire that sufficiently meets their communicative needs in the classroom, negotiation for meaning is reduced to a communication strategy that may become a limited and even debilitating strategy for developing more advanced levels of second language accuracy. Pica (1994) acknowledged that second language accuracy plays only a secondary role in negotiation, as defined in SLA research: "Negotiation, by definition, focuses on the *comprehensibility* of message meaning, and on the message's *form* only insofar as that can contribute to its comprehensibility.

Learners and their interlocutors find ways to communicate messages through negotiation, but not necessarily with target-like forms" (pp. 517–518). In the context of content-based ESL classrooms, therefore, it should come as no surprise that Pica (2002) found very little negotiation for meaning that might be expected to move second language development forward. Instead, as students and teacher negotiated for meaning to guarantee comprehensibility during discussion of film reviews, the majority of students' non-target utterances went unaddressed in any direct way: "Although there was a good deal of negotiation for meaning, the focus of the discussion was on defining unfamiliar lexical items and clarifying factual information rather than on calling attention to grammatical items" (Pica, Kang, & Sauro 2006:307).

3.3 Negotiation of form

Gass (1997) acknowledged that negotiation of form and meaning are not easily separable in dyadic interactions yet SLA researchers investigating negotiation have typically shown a categorical preference for investigating negotiation that facilitates "comprehensibility of message meaning" rather than negotiation that "can be interrupted by a correction" (Pica 1994:494–495). For negotiation to be a useful strategy for teaching language through content, however, it needs to encompass more than only strategies for sustaining communication. As was evident in Marie's lesson about the water cycle, mutual comprehension can easily be achieved in classroom interaction, despite students' use of non-target forms. For this reason, Swain (1985) argued that teachers, in order to benefit their students' interlanguage development, need to incorporate ways of "pushing" students to produce language that is not only comprehensible, but also accurate.

An argument is presented here, based on both observational and experimental studies of immersion and content-based classrooms, for investing negotiation with a pedagogical function that entails corrective feedback delivered in a way that is compatible with subject-matter instruction. Lyster and Ranta (1997) observed different feedback types that immersion teachers have at their disposal and then identified which feedback types tended more than others to "push" learners to modify their non-target output. They observed six different types of feedback: recasts, explicit correction, clarification requests, repetition of error, elicitation, and metalinguistic clues. Recasts (defined earlier in this chapter) and explicit correction both supply learners with target reformulations of their non-target output. Whereas a recast is considered implicit insofar as it contains no metalinguistic information, an explicit correction contains the correct form as well as a clear indication that what the student said was inaccurate:

> S: *Le renard gris, le loup, le coyote, le bison et la gr...groue.*
>   [The gray fox, the wolf, the coyote, the bison, and the cr...cran.]
> T: *Et la grue. On dit 'grue'.* [And the crane. We say 'crane'.]

In contrast, clarification requests, repetition of error, elicitation, and met-alinguistic clues (see next section for definitions) were grouped together as "prompts," because they withhold correct forms and instead offer learners an opportunity to self-repair by generating their own modified response (Lyster 2004a; Lyster & Mori 2006; Ranta & Lyster 2007). When a teacher's prompt is followed by a learner repair move, the teacher-student exchange is said to in-volve the "negotiation of form" (Lyster & Ranta 1997; Lochtman 2005), because it serves to hand the floor over to students while drawing attention to accuracy. Clarification requests and repetition of error also can be used to negotiate for meaning, but have the propensity to negotiate form for two reasons: They push learners to modify their non-target output (Pica et al. 1996) and they are often used by teachers, not because they misunderstand, but rather to feign incom-prehension and to intentionally draw attention to non-target forms (Lyster & Ranta 1997). Although explicit correction is also intended to draw attention to non-target forms, it does so in a way that does not allow for negotiation because, like recasts, it provides the form unilaterally and, thus, creates an op-portunity for the learner to repeat the teacher's alternative form but not to self-repair. Self-repair, therefore, results not from explicitness, but rather from the illocutionary force of prompts that are intended to engage students more dialogically. Unlike recasts and explicit correction, prompts maintain the mu-tuality inherent in negotiation by returning the floor to students along with cues to draw on their own linguistic resources.

Lyster and Mori (2006) found that teachers in French and Japanese im-mersion classrooms used these different feedback types in similar propor-tions (see Figure 2). Recasts constituted the greatest proportion of feedback in both settings (54–65%), followed by prompts (26–38%), then explicit cor-rection (7–9%). Lyster (1998b) found that French immersion teachers tended to use prompts to address lexical errors and to use recasts for grammatical and phonological errors. Overall, prompts were more effective at leading to imme-diate repair than were recasts or explicit correction, especially for lexical and grammatical errors. Phonological repairs resulted primarily from recasts.

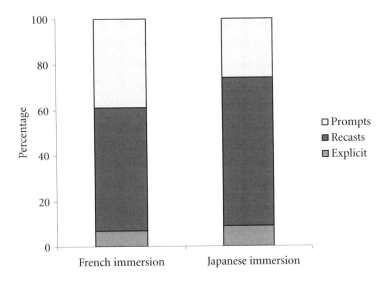

Figure 2. Percentage distribution of feedback types in immersion classrooms (Lyster & Mori 2006: 285)

3.3.1 *Prompting*

Prompts are defined below, along with examples from Grade 4 French immersion classes, all of which address grammatical gender to better illustrate differences across feedback types while maintaining consistency in error type (M = masculine; F = feminine).

– Clarification request: the teacher indicates to the student, by using phrases such as "*Pardon me*" and "*I don't understand*," that the message has not been understood or that the utterance is ill-formed in some way, and that a repetition or a reformulation is required.

> S: *La marmotte, c'est pas celui en haut?*
>   [The groundhog-F, isn't it the one-M at the top?]
> T: *Pardon?* [Excuse me?]
> S: *La marmotte, c'est pas celle en haut?*
>   [The groundhog-F, isn't it the one-F at the top?]

– Repetition: the teacher repeats the student's erroneous utterance, adjusting the intonation to highlight the error.

> S: *Puis ma grand-mère a acheté du laine pour faire euh... tu sais...* [And my grandmother bought some wool-M to make um... you know...]

> T: *Du laine?* [Wool-M?]
> S: *De la laine.* [Wool-F.]

- Metalinguistic clues: the teacher provides comments, information, or questions related to the well-formedness of the student's utterance, without explicitly providing the correct form (e.g., *"Do we say 'goed' in English?"* *"We don't say that in French,"* *"No,"* *"Is it masculine?"*).

> S: *Parce qu'elle cherche, euh, son, son carte.*
>   [Because she's looking for, um, her, her card-M.]
> T: *Pas son carte.* [Not her card-M.]
> S: *Euh, sa carte?* [Um, her card-F?]

- Elicitation: the teacher directly elicits correct forms from students by asking questions such as *"How do we say that in French?"* or by pausing to allow students to complete the teacher's utterance (e.g., *"C'est un. . . ?"*), or by asking students to reformulate their utterance (e.g., *"Try again"*).

> T: *Il vit où un animal domestique? Où est-ce que ça vit?*
>   [Where does a pet live? Where does it live?]
> S: *Dans un maison.* [In a house-M.]
> T: *Dans. . . ? Attention.* [In . . .? Careful.]
> S: *Dans une maison.* [In a house-F.]

Rachelle, a Grade 4 early immersion teacher, illustrates the use of prompts in the following exchanges observed by Lyster (1998d, 2002b). Rachelle draws attention to her students' non-target output in ways that encourage them to peer- or self-repair more so than Marie did in the exchanges about the water cycle, because her early immersion students have had more exposure to the target language than Marie's middle immersion students. The exchange is extracted from a science lesson about mammals and their natural defences against predators.

1) T:	*Le lièvre. Joseph pourrais-tu nous dire quels sont les moyens que tu vois, toi, d'après l'illustration là?*	*1) T:*	*The hare. Joseph could you tell us what are the means of defence that you see from this illustration?*
2) S1:	*Il court vite, puis il saute.*	*2) S1:*	*It runs fast and it hops.*
3) T:	*Il court vite.*	*3) T:*	*It runs fast.*
4) S2:	*Il bond.*	*4) S2:*	*It jump.*
5) T:	*Il bond?*	*5) T:*	*It jump?*

6) Ss:	*Il bondit.*		*6) Ss:*	*It jumps.*	
7) T:	*Il bondit, c'est le verbe ...?*		*7) T:*	*It jumps, from the verb...?*	
8) Ss:	*Bondir.*		*8) Ss:*	*To jump.*	
9) T:	*Bondir. Il fait des bonds. Hein, il bondit. Ensuite... [...] Le porc-épic? Sara?*		*9) T:*	*To jump. It jumps about. Right, it jumps. Next... [...] The porcupine? Sara?*	
10) S3:	*C'est les piques sur le dos. C'est...*		*10) S3:*	*It's the pines on its back. It's...*	
11) T:	*Les piques. Est-ce qu'on dit «les piques»?*		*11) T:*	*The pines. Do we say "the pines"?*	
12) S4:	*Les épiques.*		*12) S4:*	*The upines.*	
13) T:	*Les...?*		*13) T:*	*The...?*	
14) S5:	*Les piquants.*		*14) S5:*	*The quills*	
15) T:	*Les piquants, très bien. Les piquants.*		*15) T:*	*The quills, very good. The quills.*	

In turn 3, Rachelle repeats *Il court vite* ("It runs fast") to confirm one of Joseph's contributions from turn 2. Then in turn 5 she repeats the student's ill-formed utterance to draw attention to the non-target form, *Il bond ("It jump")*. Other students immediately provide the target form, *Il bondit* ("It jumps"), which Rachelle confirms by repeating in turn 7, then asks for its infinitive form. In turn 8, several students propose *bondir,* which Rachelle confirms by repeating in turn 9, then provides a synonymous phrase (*Il fait des bonds*) along with a final repetition of *Il bondit* before calling on Joseph to continue. The lesson continues, uninterrupted by Rachelle's prompt in turn 5 and the students' peer-repair move in turn 6. The topic then switches to porcupines and the precise word for "quills." In response to Sara's suggestion in turn 10 (*les piques*), Rachelle's follow-up move is a prompt combining a metalinguistic clue with repetition of the error: *Est-ce qu'on dit 'les piques'?* Another student also proposes an invented term in turn 12 (*les épiques*), which incites Rachelle to use a prompt in turn 13 (*Les...?*) that not only aims to elicit the target form but also serves as a rejection of the non-target form and, thus, as negative evidence. This simple move succeeds in eliciting *Les piquants* in turn 14, the correct term approved and repeated by Rachelle in her follow-up.

The examples of prompting in the preceding excerpt do not support claims made by Krashen (1994) and Truscott (1999) that oral feedback on accuracy causes anxiety and breaks the communicative flow, nor claims by Long (2007) that prompts interfere with the delivery of syllabus content. Because the educational objectives of this science lesson are, first, to familiarize students with a range of defence mechanisms used by specific mammals against their predators and, second, to enable students to express their understanding of these natural defence systems, it is befitting that they be pushed to use accurately the verb *bondir* ("jump") as they discuss hares, and the noun *piquants* ("quills") to discuss porcupines. Prompts fit well with instructional discourse and are especially compatible with content teaching, as they resemble the "clueing" procedure or "withholding phenomenon" identified by McHoul (1990) in his study of feedback in subject-matter classrooms. Moreover, the lively discussion about hares and porcupines enables both teacher and students to engage in collective scaffolding (Donato 1994) and allows students to test their creative hypotheses. If we remove Rachelle's prompts and associated responses, students contribute much less to the remaining exchange:

1) T:	Le lièvre. Joseph pourrais-tu nous dire quels sont les moyens que tu vois, toi, d'après l'illustration là?	1) T:	The hare. Joseph could you tell us what are the means of defense that you see from this illustration?
2) S1:	Il court vite, puis il saute.	2) S1:	It runs fast and it hops.
3) T:	Il court vite.	3) T:	It runs fast.
4) S2:	Il bond.	4) S2:	It jump.
9) T:	... Hein, il bondit. Ensuite... [...] Le porc-épic? Sara?	9) T:	... Right, it jumps. Next... [...] The porcupine? Sara?
10) S3:	C'est les piques sur le dos. C'est...	10) S3:	It's the pines on its back. It's...
15) T:	Les piquants, très bien. Les piquants.	15) T:	The quills, very good. The quills.

Without Rachelle's prompts, the students are left with only recasts, and the resulting interaction lacks the pedagogical richness and creative experimentation that enlivened the interaction with prompts. Of theoretical interest here is the propensity of prompts to draw students' attention to form while maintaining a central focus on meaning (Long 1996) and to create opportunities for transfer-appropriate learning (Segalowitz 1997).

The next exchange is also extracted from Rachelle's science lesson about how mammals are naturally predisposed to protect themselves from predators. This example serves to broaden the scope of the negotiation of form to include not only its corrective function but also its function of providing or eliciting other relevant information about language during interaction related to content. This lively exchange about skunks illustrates not only how Rachelle pushes her students to refine their vocabulary, moving from *puant* to *malodor-*

ant ("stinky" to "malodorous"), but also how she allows them to experiment with derivational morphology as they search together for the opposite of the word *odorant* ("odorous").

1) T:	*Alors la mouffette, qu'est-ce qu'elle fait, elle? Karen?*		*1) T:*	*And so the skunk, what does it do? Karen?*
2) S1:	*Um... elle jet...Bien il y a un jet de parfum qui sent pas très bon...*		*2) S1:*	*Um...it does...Well there's a stream of perfume that doesn't smell very good...*
3) T:	*Alors un jet de parfum, on va appeler ça un ...?*		*3) T:*	*So a stream of perfume that doesn't smell very good, we'll call it a ...?*
4) Ss:	*Liquide.*		*4) Ss:*	*Liquid*
5) T:	*Liquide. Un liquide ...*		*5) T:*	*Liquid. A liquid. . .*
6) S2:	*Puant.*		*6) S2:*	*Stinky*
7) T:	*Un liquide puant. Aussi on appelle ça. . . ? Un liquide qui n'a pas une bonne odeur, comment on appelle ça? Un liquide qui n'a pas une bonne odeur? Quand c'est une bonne odeur, comment on dit ça? C'est o...?*		*7) T:*	*A stinky liquid. We also call that. . . ? A liquid that does not have a good odour, how do we call that? A liquid that does not have a good odour? When it's a good odour, how do we say that? It's o. . . ?*
8) Ss:	*Odoreux?*		*8) Ss:*	*Odorful?*
9) T:	*O...do...?*		*9) T:*	*O...do...?*
10) Ss:	*Odorant?*		*10) Ss:*	*Odorous?*
11) T:	*Hein?*		*11) T:*	*What?*
12) Ss:	*Odorant.*		*12) Ss:*	*Odorous.*
13) T:	*Odorant. Et si c'est. . . ?*		*13) T:*	*Odorous. And if it's. . . ?*
14) Ss:	*Désodorant.*		*14) Ss:*	*Deodorant.*
15) T:	*Hein?*		*15) T:*	*What?*
16) Ss:	*Désodorant.*		*16) Ss:*	*Deodorant.*
17) T:	*Désodorant. [laughs]*		*17) T:*	*Deodorant. [laughs]*
18) S3:	*Désodorance?*		*18) S3:*	*Deodorance?*
19) S4:	*Inodorance?*		*19) S4:*	*Inodorance?*

20) T: In-, in-, c'est une bonne idée. «In» ça veut dire «pas». Inodorance? On va dire «malodorant».	*20) T: In-, in-, that's not a bad idea! "In" means "not." Inodorance? The word is "malodorous."*
21) S4: Ah oui.	*21) S4: Oh yeah.*

In asking students how skunks defend themselves against predators, Rachelle first elicits "a stream of perfume" (*un jet de parfum*), to which she replies with a repetition and an elicitation to prompt students to propose a more accurate term. She succeeds in eliciting the more accurate terms *liquide* and then *puant* in turns 4 and 6, respectively. In search of a stylistically more appropriate term than *puant*, Rachelle then elicits from the students the word *odorant* in order to allow them to discover its antonym, *malodorant*. Although it is Rachelle who finally provides the word *malodorant*, in the process the students propose the prefixes *dé-* and *in-*. Rachelle points out that *in-* is a particularly good idea because it means "not." This short sequence on prefixes, integrated into a spirited discussion about skunks, is an exemplary exchange, because we know from research that immersion teachers typically tend not to focus on structural information about vocabulary outside of separate grammar lessons (Allen et al. 1990) and that immersion students are limited in their productive use of such derivational morphology (Harley & King 1989; Harley 1992).

The work of Gibbons (2003), introduced earlier, considered a teacher's use of recasts as a means of scaffolding her interactions with ESL students during teacher-guided reporting in mainstream science lessons. We now return to that setting to further illustrate the effectiveness in content-based lessons of moving beyond recasting and instead pushing learners to stretch their language resources. While prompts can effectively do this as they push learners to self-repair non-target utterances, various other signals for clarification can be used effectively to encourage students to persevere in using the target language to express emergent knowledge with increasing refinement. For example, in the following teacher-student exchange from Gibbons (2003), the teacher initially signals to the student that a reformulation is necessary, and then finally supplies a reformulated version of the student's meaning, "only after the learner has had opportunities for self-correction" (p. 261):

> T: *what did you find out?*
> S: *if you put a nail . onto the piece of foil .. and then pick it . pick it up .. the magnet will . . . . that if you put a . nail under a piece of foil . and then pick . pick the foil up with the magnet .. still . still with the nail .. under it . . . it won't*

T: *it what?*

S: *it won't/ it won't come out*

T: *what won't come out?*

S: *it'll go up*

T: *wait just a minute .. can you explain that a bit more Julianna?*

S: *like if you put a nail and then foil over it and then put the nail on top . of the foil .. the nail underneath the foil/ Miss I can't say it*

T: *no you're doing fine I/ I can see*

S: *Miss forget about the magnet/ em the magnet holds it with the foil up the top and the nail's underneath and the foil's on top and put the magnet in it and you lift it up .. and the nail will em … hold it/ stick with the magnet and the foil's in between*

T: *oh/ so even with the foil in between the . magnet will <u>still</u> pick up the nail . alright does the magnet pick up the foil?*

S: *no*

This exchange illustrates how the teacher's prompting ("can you explain that a bit more Julianna?") and encouragement ("you're doing fine") push the learner to stretch her language resources: "Julianna is at the outer limits of what she can do alone. Yet, because of the precise and contingent nature of the teacher's scaffolding, the text is characterized by the student's, rather than the teacher's, reformulations" (Gibbons 2003: 262).

In the next exchange, the teacher uses an elicitation move to signal that a reformulation is necessary, "but, knowing that the learner can achieve it alone, she hands the responsibility over to the student" (Gibbons 2003: 263).

T: *tell us what you found out*

S: *we found out that the south and the south don't like to stick together*

T: *now let's/ let's start using our scientific language Michelle*

S: *the north and the north repelled each other and the south and the south also .. repelled each other but when we put the/ when we put the two magnets in a different way they/ they attracted each other*

This example illustrates how the teacher's elicitation of more appropriate language ("let's start using our scientific language") results in longer and more complete learner discourse than does a recast, an important outcome for teachers to consider when selecting feedback to encourage students to increase and to refine their use of the target language.

3.3.2 *Self-repair*

Increasingly handing the floor over to students is an integral part of scaffolding, which aims to enable learners to take more and more responsibility for their own learning, as "an interpersonal process is transformed into an intrapersonal one" (Vygotsky 1978:57). The shift from other-regulation to self-regulation is slow to happen in many classrooms, however, where there is a heavy emphasis on other-repair (e.g., Van Lier 1988), in contrast to non-classroom settings where self-repair predominates (Schegloff, Jefferson, & Sacks 1977). Van Lier (1988) suggested that other-repair (e.g., when a teacher recasts a learner's utterance) "may deny the speaker the opportunity to do self-repair, probably an important learning activity" (p. 211). He argued that postponing other-repair in favour of more self-repair would "promote the development of self-monitoring and pragmatic adjustment which is essential to competence in the target language" (p. 211). Similarly, Aljaafreh and Lantolf (1994) emphasized the importance of the novice moving away from reliance on the expert's other-repair and toward more reliance on the self: "For this to happen, however, the expert must be willing to relinquish control (itself dialogically negotiated) to the novice at the appropriate time" (p. 480). Swain (1985, 1988, 1993) too argued in favour of ample opportunities for student production and the provision of feedback to push students to express themselves more precisely and appropriately. In fact, since some of the earliest classroom-based studies on corrective feedback, many researchers have maintained that pushing learners in their output, rather than providing them with correct forms, is likely to benefit their interlanguage development (e.g., Allwright 1975; Allwright & Bailey 1991; Chaudron 1988; Hendrickson 1978; Vigil & Oller 1976). For example, Corder (1967:168) wrote:

> simple provision of the correct form may not always be the only, or indeed the most effective form of error correction since it bars the way to the learner testing alternative hypotheses. Making a learner try to discover the right form could often be more instructive to both learner and teacher.

Support for self-repair can also be found in studies of educational contexts other than those dealing specifically with second language learning. For example, Lepper, Aspinwall, Mumme, and Chabay (1990) found that expert tutors rarely give students correct answers, except as a last resort, and, instead, offer students hints in the form of questions or remarks.

With the aim of examining corrective feedback in terms of its illocutionary force, Lyster and Ranta (1997) borrowed the term "uptake" from speech act theory (see Austin 1962; Levinson 1983; Mey 1993) to refer to the range of possible utterances made by students in response to corrective feedback. The notion of uptake in classroom studies provides a tool for identifying patterns in teacher-student interaction that include various responses following teacher feedback, thus allowing for an operationalization of "pushed output" (Swain 1985, 1988). In earlier work, "learner uptake" referred to "what learners claim to have learned from a particular lesson" (Slimani 1992; see also Allwright 1984), and "teacher uptake" referred to teacher questions that incorporate part of a student's preceding contribution (Collins 1982). Lyster and Ranta's (1997) use of the term has since been used in studies of classroom interaction that include investigations of French immersion classrooms (Lyster 1998b), Japanese immersion classrooms (Mori 2000, 2002), English immersion classrooms (Lee 2006), ESL classrooms (Ellis et al. 2001; Panova & Lyster 2002), EFL classrooms (Havranek 2002; Sheen 2004; Tsang 2004), and Belgian classrooms in which German is taught as a foreign language (Lochtman 2002, 2005). Lyster and Ranta's data-driven "error treatment sequence," which includes a range of feedback types in addition to various types of learner uptake, has proven useful in descriptive studies of feedback that are concerned not only with feedback itself but also with the range of possible learner responses to feedback. It has been used with some variation (e.g., Ellis et al. 2001) and has helped to reveal unexpected differences across instructional settings that will be further discussed in the next chapter.

Lyster and Ranta (1997) were not the first (nor the last) to quantify learner responses immediately following feedback (e.g., Brock et al. 1986; Chaudron 1977; Doughty 1994; Gass & Varonis 1989; Oliver 1995). Long (2007) criticized their use of the term 'uptake' but misconstrued immediate uptake as an instance of acquisition, even though other researchers have not suggested that uptake is a measure of acquisition. In fact, researchers have been quick to dispel false hopes that either the learner's repetition of the correct form or the use of alternative forms following feedback can be considered as evidence of learning (e.g., Corder 1967; Gass 1988; Gass & Varonis 1994; Mackey & Philp 1998; Schachter 1983). Instead, researchers tend to regard uptake as "related to learners' perceptions about feedback at the time of feedback" (Mackey et al. 2000: 492), as "evidence that learners are noticing the feedback" (Lightbown 2000: 447), or as "facilitative of acquisition" (Ellis et al. 2001). Because uptake alone does not constitute learning, it is important to examine the effects of interactional feedback and learner repair on long-term second language development (see next section). Second language learning is a complex and time-consuming process that cannot be reduced to a learner's immediate response to corrective feedback, but different types of repair are likely to affect second language development differentially over time because different types of repair trigger different types of processing.

Learner uptake includes either (a) utterances still in need of repair or (b) utterances with repair. Unlike studies of conversational analysis (e.g., Kasper 1985; Schegloff et al. 1977), repair in this context refers to the correct reformulation of an error in a single student turn and not to the whole sequence of turns resulting in the correct reformulation. When analyzing the potential effects of different types of feedback, learner responses with repair are of greater interest than responses still in need of repair, but not because immediate repair is an instance of acquisition or a guarantee of subsequent acquisition. Of significance instead is the distinction between two types of immediate repair that analyses of uptake have made clear: Recasts and explicit correction can lead only to repetition of correct forms by students, whereas prompts can lead, not to repetition, but either to self-repair or peer-repair. Self-repair following a prompt arguably requires a deeper level of processing than repetition of a teacher's recast. Self-repair is thus more likely to destabilize interlanguage forms, as learners are pushed to reanalyze interlanguage representations and to attend to the retrieval of alternative forms. In contrast to self-repair following prompts, repetition of a recast does not engage learners in a similarly deep level of processing nor necessitates any reanalysis. In the case of peer-repair, although the student who actually produces the initial error does not self-repair, the salience of a target form and thus the conditions for its being noticed are arguably greater when the form is provided by peers after a teacher's prompt, because of the ensuing negative evidence, than when the form is embedded in a teacher's recast.

Designing practice activities that are both communicative in purpose and controlled in the sense of requiring the use of specific target forms is an instructional challenge addressed in the preceding chapter. This is where prompts play a central role. Given their aim to elicit modified output, prompts serve to scaffold opportunities for controlled practice in the context of communicative interaction. As with other types of practice, prompts aim to improve control over already-internalized forms by providing opportunities for "pushed" output, hypothesized by Swain (1985, 1988) to move interlanguage development forward, and by assisting learners in the transition from declarative to procedural knowledge (de Bot 1996; DeKeyser 1998; Lyster & Ranta 1997; Ranta & Lyster 2007). Learners can be prompted, therefore, only to retrieve knowledge that already exists in some form (e.g., declarative knowledge; see Lyster & Ranta 1997). This is feasible in immersion and content-based classrooms where learners have presumably been exposed to masses of input through subject-matter instruction, resulting in the encoding of ample target language knowledge that continues to be accessible for comprehension but that requires further activation before becoming part of a learner's productive repertoire. De Bot (1996) argued that second language learners will benefit more from being pushed to retrieve target language forms than from merely hearing the forms in the input, because retrieval and subsequent production stimulate the development of connections in memory. Long (2007) challenged the psycholinguistic rationale for prompting, however, arguing that "acquisition of new knowledge is the major goal, not 'automatizing' the retrieval of existing knowledge" (p. 102). However, the ultimate goal of instruction is not to continuously present only new knowledge to students, without sufficiently providing subsequent opportunities for assimilation and consolidation of that knowledge. In school-based learning, students need repeated opportunities to retrieve and restructure their knowledge of the target language through a "cyclical" or "spiral" syllabus, whereby "new subject matter should not be introduced once in a syllabus and then dropped; rather, it should be reintroduced in different manifestations at various times" (Dubin & Olshtain 1986: 55; see also Allen 1983; Cameron 2001; Rutherford 1987; Skehan 1998; Stern 1992). For classroom learners to engage in a sufficiently deep level of processing that will strengthen connections between recently encoded representations in long-term memory and actual language production, one instance of encoding without further activation via external prompting is obviously insufficient and not upheld by educators, nor most researchers, as an instance of acquisition. For example, Skehan (1998) argued for a cyclical syllabus that would

> revisit aspects of the emerging interlanguage syllabus regularly to enable newly analysed or newly lexicalized material to be integrated into the developing system. The cyclical nature of the syllabus would avoid the situation of allowing only one chance for this to occur – learning and development are not so conveniently precise and packageable.   (p. 92)

Prompting and other techniques for negotiating language through content provide effective ways of revisiting target items and grammatical subsystems in ways that encourage the gradual development of a network of meaningful associations that become increasingly accessible for learners during communicative interaction.

3.4 Classroom intervention studies

In a recent classroom study of adult ESL learners, Ellis, Lowen, and Erlam (2006) compared the effects of recasts versus prompts on students' use of the simple past tense in English. Operationalizing prompts as a repetition plus a metalinguistic clue, they found significantly superior effects for prompts over recasts on delayed post-test measures. Similarly, Havranek and Cesnik (2001) found repair following prompts to be the most effective feedback combination in a range of EFL classrooms. At least three other classroom studies have also demonstrated that oral feedback, especially in the form of prompts, has a significant effect on second language development in elementary school settings involving content-based ESL, French immersion, and communicative ESL. These are described below.

In Doughty and Varela's (1998) study of two content-based ESL classrooms, students in one classroom received corrective feedback on both simple and conditional past tense forms during science activities, while students in the other classroom engaged in the same science activities, but without feedback. Two types of feedback, together called "corrective recasting," were used in sequence: first, the teacher repeated the student's non-target utterance, drawing attention to the error with stress and rising intonation; second, if the learner failed to respond, the teacher provided a recast in which the verb form was stressed (see Long 2007, for a completely different definition of corrective recasts). The teacher's use of "corrective recasts" was arguably at odds with the researchers' characterization of the double-feedback move as an "implicit focus on form" (p. 118) that was only "slightly more explicit than recasts" (p. 124). The class receiving feedback showed significant improvement in comparison to the class receiving no feedback at all, and maintained this advantage two months later. Students appeared especially to benefit from the teacher's repetition of their non-target utterances, as evidenced by the observation that, by the beginning of the second of three treatment sessions, "students were beginning to self-correct before the teacher had the opportunity to recast" (p. 135; see Lyster 1998a, for similar evidence that repetition of a student's error provided in tandem with other types of feedback is a particularly effective combination yielding high rates of immediate repair). Because the teacher consistently used repetition to draw attention to the error and then recast only when students made no attempt at repair, the study provides more support for prompting techniques than for recasting, a finding that was further substantiated in two subsequent classroom studies.

Lyster (2004a) examined the differential effects of prompts and recasts in his form-focused intervention study described earlier. In addition to the instructional unit on grammatical gender, the three Grade 5 immersion teachers each interacted with students in a specific way that permitted comparisons of three oral feedback options: prompts, recasts, and no feedback. The comparison group received no form-focused instruction nor any preplanned feedback on grammatical gender. The analysis of eight proficiency measures (i.e., two oral tasks and two written tasks administered immediately following the instructional unit and then again two months later) showed that the group receiving prompts distinguished itself by being the only group to significantly outperform the comparison group on all eight measures. The recast group significantly outperformed the comparison group on five of the eight measures, while the instruction-only group (receiving no feedback) significantly outperformed the comparison group on four of the eight measures, suggesting that recasts were more effective than no feedback, but only marginally so.

Ammar and Spada (2006) also investigated the differential effects of prompts and recasts in form-focused instruction in three Grade 6 intensive ESL classrooms over a four-week period. The form-focused intervention targeted third-person possessive determiners in English (*his* and *her*), which are known to be difficult for francophone learners of English even after many years of ESL instruction (White 1998). Students in all three classes received form-focused instruction, which included metalinguistic information and both controlled and communicative practice activities. During the practice activities, one class received feedback in the form of recasts, another received prompts, and the third received no feedback. Results of pre-tests, immediate post-tests, and delayed post-tests showed that all three groups benefited from the form-focused instruction, and that the two feedback groups benefited the most, both outperforming the control group on immediate and delayed oral post-tests. The group receiving prompts significantly outperformed the recast group on written and oral post-tests. Prompts were especially effective for lower-proficiency learners, whereas higher-proficiency learners appeared to benefit similarly from both recasts and prompts.

The findings of the intervention studies by Lyster (2004a), Ammar and Spada (2006), and Ellis et al. (2006) indicate that learners who are prompted to retrieve more target-like forms are more likely to retrieve these forms during subsequent processing than learners merely hearing recasts of these forms. Important to reiterate is that these studies all included measures of target language development over time rather than considering immediate learner responses. Otherwise, given the ostensibly binary nature of target features such as gender attribution in French and possessive determiners in English, the rate of immediate repair could arguably have been affected by a seemingly simple on-the-spot computation (i.e., if *his* is wrong then it must be *her*). Whether or not learners could be easily led in this way to repair their errors immediately following feedback, however, was not used as a measure of effectiveness in these intervention studies. Instead, whether or not learners could retrieve more target-like forms at a later point in time was examined.

The effectiveness of prompts is arguably related to the opportunities for meaningful practice they create, pushing learners to retrieve newly acquired forms during online production. When the instructional goal is to assist learners in the transition from declarative to procedural knowledge, providing learners with opportunities to engage with feedback in a productive mode via prompting is arguably more effective than engaging students in a more receptive mode via recasting. The results of research on the "generation effect" also predict, for similar reasons, that prompts will be more effective than recasts. This line of experimental research has consistently found that learners remember information better when they take an active part in producing it, rather than having it provided by an external source (e.g., Clark 1995; deWinstanley & Bjork 2004). That learners benefited less from recasting may also be due to the difficulty learners have in noticing recasts of morphosyntactic errors (Carpenter et al. 2006; Lyster 1998b; Mackey et al. 2000). It seems likely as well that students receiving prompts developed more "feedback appreciation" (Skehan 1998) as a result of increased opportunities for conscious awareness of their teacher's feedback and were thus more predisposed towards a rule-based perspective, which in turn led to robust changes in their rule-based representations. That is, conscious awareness of feedback ("consciousness enhanced processing") predisposes learners towards a rule-based perspective, which in turn is more likely to lead to longer-term change (Skehan 1998). Similarly, Ellis et al. (2006) concluded with respect to metalinguistic feedback that its effectiveness "might derive in part from the high level of awareness it generates and in part from the fact that it is embedded in a communicative context" (p. 363).

4.   Counterbalanced feedback

Long (2007) recommended the use of only one type of feedback – recasts – at the expense of all others. Yet, at the same time, he acknowledged that a case for the superiority of recasts to other forms of feedback has not yet been "definitively made – far from it" (p. 103). He referred to those with empirical data that oppose his theoretical view as "sceptics" (p. 94) whose "doubt" he sees as a "challenge to the optimism about recasts" (p. 104). In contrast, the intention of this chapter has been to depict an array of feedback options that teachers have at their disposal – precisely so they can move away from overusing one type of corrective feedback (i.e., recasts) over another. That recent classroom studies demonstrated superior effects for prompts over recasts should by no means be construed as an argument for their exclusive use. The findings are promising and indeed challenge Long's rigid position, but should be used instead to support a balanced mix of prompts and recasts.

Lyster and Mori (2006) argued that learners are likely to notice the corrective quality of a good number of recasts, depending on the interactional context (see also Oliver & Mackey 2003), especially in cases where the recasts have been shortened and/or provided with added stress to highlight the error. Also beneficial are recasts provided by a teacher to scaffold interaction during subject-matter instruction when target forms are beyond a learner's current abilities. As Nicholas et al. (2001) concluded, however, "there is a point beyond which recasts are ineffective in changing stabilized interlanguages" (p. 752). Beyond such a point, learners will benefit more from being pushed to produce modified output by means of prompting, especially in cases where recasts could be perceived ambiguously as approving their use of non-target forms and where learners have reached a developmental plateau in their use of the non-target forms. Prompts may be particularly beneficial in communicatively-oriented and content-based classrooms where learners have many opportunities to communicate but have a tendency to do so with a classroom code easily understood by both teacher and peers. In these contexts, negotiating for comprehensibility and continued recasting of what students already know are unlikely to be effective strategies for ensuring continued development of target language accuracy. Similarly, continued prompting of learners to draw on what they have not yet acquired will be equally ineffective.

Decisions about whether to provide recasts or prompts need also to take into account the students' familiarity with the content of the lesson. That is, interaction about content with which students are unfamiliar is propitious for the use of recasts, whereas interaction about content familiar to students provides ideal opportunities for the use of prompts (Lyster 1998d). Teachers are often reluctant to draw attention to language during informal conversations initiated by students, seeing them as good opportunities for students to express themselves freely without the constraints of formal feedback. However, these moments are ideal for providing helpful feedback precisely because students are in complete control of the content. Some of the most effective teachers may be those who are willing and able to orchestrate, in accordance with their students' language abilities and content familiarity, a wide range of feedback types befitting of the instructional context. The next chapter further explores the counterbalancing act in which immersion and content-based teachers need to engage as they integrate language and content during their instructional day and throughout the school year.

CHAPTER 5

Counterbalanced instruction

This book began by identifying a range of instructional settings in which subject matter is used at least some of the time as a means for students to learn an additional language. The rationale for adopting content-based instruction over more traditional language instruction is well-founded in that subject-matter instruction provides the cognitive basis for second language learning, as well as the requisite motivational basis for purposeful communication (Snow et al. 1989). In support of content-based instruction, research on Canadian immersion programs was highlighted, because of the extent and range of the research undertaken in those settings. Results over the past 40 years have repeatedly shown that what Lightbown and Spada (2006) called the "two for one" approach is successful: Immersion students who study subject matter through their second language attain the same levels of academic achievement and first language development as non-immersion students, and they attain significantly higher levels of second language proficiency than do non-immersion students studying the second language as a regular subject for one lesson per day. Wesche and Skehan (2002:227) attributed the success of immersion to the comprehensive environment it creates for second language development, characterized by intensive exposure to highly contextualized and relevant language, a motivating purpose for language learning, and a naturalistic learning context.

In comparison to native speakers, the second language proficiency of immersion students is characterized by high levels of comprehension abilities and functional levels of communicative ability in production, with shortcomings in terms of accurate and idiomatic expression, lexical variety, and sociolinguistic appropriateness. These shortcomings were explained in terms of the processing constraints that result from a complex interaction among the structural properties of certain target features, their occurrence (or non-occurrence) in typical content-based input, and the learner's own cognitive predisposition and developing system of linguistic representations. It was argued that many shortcomings in proficiency could be overcome through instructional practices that systematically integrate language and content instead of separating them. That is, classroom observation studies revealed that a typical way to approach content-based instruction is to focus exclusively on content and to refer to language only incidentally as the need arises by chance. Then, if more attention to language is called for, a traditional approach is adopted in language arts classes to engage in structural analyses of the target language out of context. A case has been made throughout this book for eschewing this non-integrated approach and instead for integrating form-focused and content-based instruction through counterbalanced instruction. With its goal of integrating both form-focused and content-based instruction in conjunction with language across the curriculum and other pivotal literacy-based approaches at the heart of school-based learning, counterbalanced instruction promotes continued second language growth by inciting learners to shift their attentional focus in a way that balances their awareness of getting two for one, that is, learning both language and content together.

1.   Why a counterbalanced approach?

The counterbalance hypothesis predicts that interlanguage restructuring is triggered by instructional interventions that orient learners in the direction opposite to that which their target language learning environment has accustomed them (Lyster & Mori 2006; see Chapter 1). The counterbalance hypothesis is predicated on Skehan's (1998) argument for pushing learners who are either form-oriented or meaning-oriented in the opposite direction in order to strike a balance between the two orientations:

> In the case of analytic learners, the intention is to build in a greater concern for fluency and the capacity to express meanings in real time without becoming excessively concerned with a focus on form. ... In the case of memory-oriented learners, the intention is to set limits to the natural tendency to prioritize communicative outcome above all else.   (pp. 171–172)

Lyster and Mori extended Skehan's argument beyond the level of individual learners to account for groups of learners whose learning styles and expectations have been shaped to a large extent by the overall communicative orientation of their classroom setting. As proposed in Chapter 1, the destabilization of interlanguage forms, in the case of learners in immersion and content-based classrooms, is hypothesized to result from instruction that requires them to vary their attentional focus between the content to which they usually attend in classroom discourse and target language features that are not otherwise attended to. The effort extended to shift attention between form and meaning in this way, and to maintain a recursive interplay, is expected to strengthen connections in memory and, thus, to facilitate access to newly analyzed or reanalyzed representations during online production. The rationale for counterbalanced instruction is now further expounded in the light of classroom research on proactive and reactive approaches to form-focused instruction.

1.1 Support from research on proactive approaches

Support for counterbalanced instruction derives in part from comparing the instructional activities and variable learning outcomes resulting from form-focused intervention studies conducted in French immersion classrooms and discussed throughout this book (see Table 3 in Chapter 2). Recall that the instructional treatment targeting two forms of the past tense in Harley's (1989) study yielded short-term improvement on two of the three measures, but no long-term significant improvement on any measures. Form-focused instruction on the conditional mood in Day and Shapson's (1991) study yielded short- and long-term significant improvement in written production, but none in oral production. In contrast, the studies targeting verbs of motion (Wright 1996), second-person pronouns (Lyster 1994a), and grammatical gender (Harley 1998; Lyster 2004a) generally yielded more positive short- and long-term results.

Norris and Ortega (2000) argued that much research on form-focused instruction has been designed in ways that favour the effectiveness of explicit treatments by using measures that require "the application of explicit declarative knowledge under controlled conditions, without much requirement for fluent, spontaneous use of contextualized language" (p. 486). In the case of the aforementioned immersion intervention studies, however, proficiency development over time was assessed by similar measures, including a range of pencil-and-paper tasks in addition to spontaneous oral production tasks. More likely to have resulted in variable outcomes are the selected target features themselves, which stem from such different linguistic domains. The functional distinctions expressed by perfective and imperfective past tenses, as well as the hypothetical meanings expressed by the conditional mood, are arguably more complex than the lexical focus on verbs of motion or the ostensibly binary distinctions apparent in grammatical gender and second-person pronouns. However, the appropriate choice of second-person pronouns is not simply binary when we factor in the complexity of social variables that learners need to take into account and the effects of pronoun choice on morphosyntax within and across sentences. Similarly, although gender attribution might seem on the surface to entail simple binary choices, it involves multiple computations in production that affect morphosyntax within and across sentences and that result from quick and discriminating access to numerous associative patterns stored in long-term memory. Notwithstanding the probability that target forms from different linguistic domains are more or less amenable to form-focused instruction (see Schwartz 1993; Spada 1997; Williams & Evans 1998), an argument is made below that the different learning outcomes yielded by these studies are the result of different emphases in the instructional treatments.

In the two studies targeting verb tenses, the emphasis on negotiation for meaning along with intrinsically motivating content-based activities arguably did not push students to notice and to use the target verb forms more accurately. That is, the main thematic activities in these studies – the creation of childhood albums and the design of futuristic space colonies – may not have created contexts that were sufficiently different from other immersion activities. By focusing students on meaningful interaction and motivating content, the instructional units may not have drawn learners' attention to linguistic accuracy any more than is typically the case and, as noted earlier, fell short of pushing students to actually use the target forms in oral production (Day & Shapson 1991). In addition, the instructional treatment in Day and Shapson's study arguably over-emphasized production activities at the expense of noticing and awareness activities. In contrast, of considerable importance in the treatments targeting verbs of motion, second-person pronouns, and gender were the noticing tasks accentuating the salience of target forms through typographical enhancement and increased frequency, followed by awareness tasks that drew students' attention to contrasts between French and English (Lyster 1994a), contrasts between interlanguage and target language forms (Wright 1996), and word-internal structural patterns (Harley 1998; Lyster 2004a). In addition, the production activities in these four studies were limited to role-plays, games, riddles, rhymes, and songs, giving more emphasis to controlled practice than to communicative practice. The games and riddles in Harley's (1998) and Lyster's (2004a) studies, for example, required students to produce target nouns and their gender-specific articles as lexicalized chunks.

Production practice that was more form-focused than meaning-focused was likely more effective across these six studies because of the selected areas of difficulty, all of which were well-known sources of persistent error. Continued opportunities for the same type of meaning-oriented interaction so characteristic of content-based classroom discourse is unlikely to change students' use of easily accessible and recalcitrant interlanguage forms (Ranta & Lyster 2007). In contrast, controlled production activities with role plays and games, in tandem with greater emphasis on noticing and awareness tasks designed to draw attention to the formal properties of target forms, led to more robust change. Arguably, the significant improvement resulted from form-focused activities that maintained conditions for transfer-appropriate learning while distinguishing themselves from other instructional activities going on at the same time in other parts of the immersion curriculum and, thus, required a shift in attention from meaning to form. With respect to language features that have reached a developmental plateau, therefore, the effectiveness of proactive instructional interventions may depend on the extent to which they are *different* from the classroom's overall communicative orientation, as long as the principles of transfer-appropriate learning are not violated. Not predicted to yield similarly positive results, therefore, are sudden injections of decontextualized grammar instruction, because of its non-integrated approach which engenders and sustains a disjunction between the processing required for encoding at the time of learning and the processing required for retrieval during communication (see Chapter 2).

1.2 Support from research on reactive approaches

As discussed in the preceding chapter, immediate repair after feedback does not constitute an instance of language learning; nevertheless, different types of repair (repetition vs. self-repair) entail different retrieval processes that contribute differentially to language development over time. In particular, self-repair triggered by prompts requires a deeper level of processing, leaving traces in memory that facilitate subsequent retrieval, more so than repetition following recasts. Recent intervention studies have shown the superiority of prompts over recasts (Ammar & Spada 2006; Ellis et al. 2006; Lyster 2004a), owing arguably to the different kinds of processing triggered by prompts and recasts. However, at least three other studies suggest that learner repetitions of recasts may also be reliable indicators of noticing and even good predictors of learning: (a) in a laboratory setting, Mackey et al. (2000) found that when learners repeated a recast they were more likely to have correctly perceived its corrective intention; (b) in EFL classrooms, Havranek and Cesnik (2001) demonstrated through follow-up language tests that recasts eliciting immediate repetition by learners were more effective than recasts not eliciting immediate repetition; and (c) in adult ESL classroom settings, Loewen (2005) showed that learner repetition of recasts was an indicator of subsequent learning. It could be the case, therefore, that prompts are more effective than recasts in a given instructional setting, because of the immediate repair they encourage. Recasts, however, might prove equally effective in another instructional setting where they too lead to immediate repair, notwithstanding findings from at least one laboratory study demonstrating that whether or not advanced learners repeat recasts in the context of dyadic interaction does not have variable effects on language development (Mackey & Philp 1998).

Lyster and Mori (2006) conducted a comparative study of reactive form-focused instruction in French and Japanese immersion classrooms in order to reveal contextual variables that might incite students to repeat recasts more in one classroom setting than in another. Their study followed descriptive classroom studies revealing discrepancies in the extent to which recasts were repeated. Specifically, infrequent repair followed recasts in French immersion classrooms in Canada (Lyster & Ranta 1997), English immersion classrooms in Korea (Lee 2006), adult ESL classrooms in Canada (Panova & Lyster 2002), and EFL classrooms in Hong Kong secondary schools (Tsang 2004), whereas more frequent repair followed recasts in Japanese immersion classrooms in the US (Mori 2002), adult ESL classrooms in New Zealand (Ellis et al. 2001), and adult EFL conversation classes in Korea (Sheen 2004).

As mentioned in the previous chapter, Lyster and Mori (2006) found that teachers in French and Japanese immersion classrooms used feedback in similar ways. However, the effects of recasts on immediate repair were different in the two settings. As seen in Figure 3, the greatest proportion of repair in Japanese immersion settings followed recasts, whereas the greatest proportion of repair in French immersion settings followed prompts. How students typically responded to recasts in each setting is illustrated by the following examples from Lyster and Mori (pp. 291–292). In the first exchange extracted from a French immersion classroom, after the teacher's recast of a student's error in choice of auxiliary and tense, the student simply continues recounting his March break activities without repeating the recast:

S: *Nous sommes allés au Biodôme*   S: *We went to the Biodome because*
    parce que ma grand-mère elle a   *my grandmother never goed to*
    jamais allé à là-bas.   *there.*
T: *Elle était jamais allée.*   T: *She had never gone.*
S: *Puis on a allé à /Jungle Adventure/*   S: *Then we goed to Jungle Adventure*
    et on a gagné des prix.   *and we won prizes.*
T: *C'est quoi ça?*   T: *What is that?*

Not only does the student not repeat the teacher's recast, he continues and makes a similar error, which the teacher ignores and instead asks the student to elaborate on the content of his message. In contrast, in the following ex-

change extracted from a Japanese immersion classroom, the teacher recasts a
student's utterance containing several grammatical errors. The student immediately repeats the recast, after which the teacher proceeds to reformulate all the
student's initial turn and then to elaborate ("So they don't put it in the house")
before concluding with a comprehension check (note that words appearing in
parentheses are necessary for the English translation but do not occur as such
in Japanese).

S: *Basha o irete to, um, um,*   S: *(They) put the wagon in it and, um,*
    toreeru ni mottearimasu.   *um, have had (it) into the trail.*
T: *Ikimasu, motteikimasu.*   T: *(They) go, (they) take (it) to the trail.*
S: *Motteikimasu.*   S: *(They) take (it) to the trail.*
T: *Basha no naka ni irete toreeru* T: *(They) put (it) in the wagon and take*
    ni motteiku. Dakara ie no naka   *(it) to the trail. So (they) don't put*
    ni okimasen. Wakaru?   *(it) in the house. Do (you)*
                                          understand?

Lyster and Mori attributed the effectiveness of recasts at eliciting immediate repair in the Japanese immersion classrooms to instructional features with
an analytic orientation, detected by means of the COLT observation scheme
(Spada & Fröhlich 1995). That is, students in Japanese immersion classrooms
occasionally engaged in choral repetition and activities that emphasized speaking as an isolated skill practiced through repetition and reading aloud – activities which likely served to prime students for repeating their teachers' recasts. These analytic features revealed a form-focused orientation that Lyster
and Mori argued, from the perspective of anglophone learners of Japanese,
resulted from specific characteristics of the target language – a typologically
different, non-cognate foreign language – that served to focus the attention
of both teachers and students more on form than would a typologically similar, cognate second language such as French. Other factors that may also have
contributed to a form-focused orientation in Japanese immersion classrooms
were the teachers' beliefs and behavior as shaped by their professional training
and cultural background. The multifaceted and inherently cultural nature of
immersion and content-based classrooms (and second language classrooms in
general; see Seedhouse 2004) makes it impossible to prescribe indiscriminately
only one type of feedback across all instructional settings. Instead, feedback
choices need to be made in accordance with specific interactional contexts,
as argued in the preceding chapter, as well as with a classroom's overriding
communicative orientation, as illustrated below. Instructional counterbalance

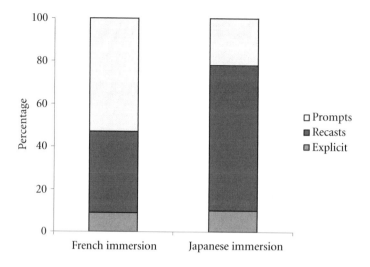

Figure 3. Percentage distribution of repair across feedback types in immersion classrooms (Lyster & Mori 2006: 286)

provides a framework for facilitating this otherwise complex process of online decision-making.

Learners in form-oriented classrooms with regular opportunities for focused production practice and an emphasis on accuracy are primed to notice the corrective function of recasts – that is, to notice the gap between their non-target output and the teacher's recast and to follow up with a repair move. In these classrooms, recasts have the potential to play unequivocally their double role as both corrective and pragmatic moves, as they draw attention to form on the one hand and confirm or disconfirm the veracity of the learner's utterance on the other. As discourse moves that are well suited to meaningful interaction, recasts enable learners in form-oriented classrooms to reorient their attentional resources towards meaning in ways that avert an overemphasis on form at the expense of meaning. This is important because, while learners who bias their attentional resources toward linguistic form benefit from their ability to detect formal distinctions, their attention to form may jeopardize their ability to process other equally important aspects of the input (Tomlin & Villa 1994). In more meaning-oriented classrooms, however, when students' attention is focused on meaning via recasting, they remain focused on meaning, not form, because they expect the teacher's immediate response to confirm or disconfirm the veracity of their utterances. In these settings, prompts – as interactional moves aiming overtly to draw learners' attention to their non-target output – enable teachers to draw students' attention to form and momentarily away from meaning. In meaning-oriented classrooms that do not usually provide opportunities for controlled production practice with an emphasis on accuracy, learners may detect the overtly corrective function of prompts more easily than the covert signals they need to infer from recasts, and they will benefit from processing the target language through the production of modified output in the form of self-repair. In the absence of opportunities for isolated oral production practice, prompts enable learners to engage productively in opportunities for elicited practice during meaningful interaction.

2. Engaging with language across the curriculum

Counterbalanced instruction promotes transfer-appropriate learning through activities that differ from a classroom's usual instructional routine. Counterbalanced instruction thus extends the scope of form-focused instruction by encompassing instructional practices that range from form-focused interventions at one end of the spectrum to content-based interventions at the other. Counterbalanced instruction is designed to encourage students to "engage with language" regardless of whether its orientation is more form-focused or more content-based. It is not only form-focused activities that incite learners to engage with language; content-based activities can also do so if they integrate or complement form-focused activities so that language permeates instructional activities across the curriculum. Students in content-based classrooms need to do so much more than briefly and fortuitously "focus on form" as they (paradoxically) "negotiate for meaning" and exchange information with a "more competent interlocutor" (Long 1996:451). More importantly, they need to engage with language through content-based instructional practices designed to stimulate their awareness of its diverse semiotic and social functions, and especially its pivotal function as a cognitive tool for learning. Eschewing focus-on-form approaches "that view language acquisition as the accumulation of sets of structures and rules," Schleppegrell et al. (2004:70) advocated content-based approaches that emphasize "how the linguistic features of disciplinary texts construe particular kinds of meanings." "No language," they argued, "is ever taught in isolation from content" (p. 68). Similarly, Handscombe (1990) proposed that, in an instructional approach that truly integrates experiential and analytic strategies, "no content is taught without reference to the language through which that content is expressed, and no language is taught without being contextualized within a thematic and human environment" (p. 185).

Drawing on Handscombe's vision of integration, counterbalanced instruction can be deployed to reverse the trend that keeps content teaching and language teaching separate. Agreeing with Swain (1988) that not all content teaching is necessarily good language teaching, Handscombe (1990) argued that "the best content teaching is also the best language teaching" (p. 185).

Counterbalanced instruction systematically integrates both content-based and form-focused instructional options. The instructional options depicted in Figure 4 encapsulate those that have been considered throughout this book as key components of pedagogy designed to enable learners to process and negotiate language across the curriculum. Content-based instructional options include: (a) techniques that teachers employ to make subject matter comprehensible to second language learners; (b) opportunities for students to use the second language to mediate content learning during academic tasks; (c) negotiation replete with questions and feedback employed by teachers to scaffold verbal exchanges with students in ways that ensure their participation and appropriation of the targeted content. Form-focused instructional options include: (a) noticing and awareness activities designed to make input features salient and to facilitate their intake in declarative form; (b) production practice activities designed to facilitate the proceduralization of target language knowledge; (c) negotiation involving teacher prompts and other engaging feedback that push students to draw optimally on their developing knowledge of the target language and increasingly to take responsibility for their learning.

Content-based and form-focused instructional options appear as discrete options in Figure 4. In the spirit of instructional counterbalance, however, content-based and form-focused instructional options are expected to interact with one another in dialectical fashion and in complementary ways. In keeping with Stern's (1990, 1992) recommendation, analytic and experiential instructional options are best seen, not as dichotomous, but as complementary pairs along a continuum. Moreover, the vertical orientation of Figure 4 is not intended to depict any hierarchical or linear relationships among instructional options that differentially emphasize input, production, and negotiation. That is, content-based and form-focused instructional options need to be counterbalanced to promote shifts in learners' attentional focus through activities that interweave balanced opportunities for input, production, and negotiation. Teachers can counterbalance instructional options across the curriculum by interweaving learning activities that vary from more content-based to more form-focused. By orchestrating a diverse range of opportunities for processing and negotiating language across the curriculum, teachers trigger the requisite

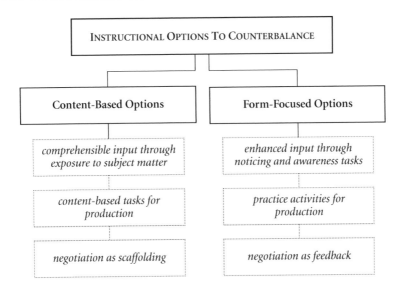

Figure 4. Instructional options to counterbalance

shifts in learner attention that are predicted by the counterbalance hypothesis to ensure continued second language growth.

Input-based instruction generally precedes production-based activities in typical content-based programs, but this is so only in the initial stages. As students progress through the program, input-based and production-based instructional activities increasingly become inextricably linked, as the ability to both comprehend subject matter and communicate about it effectively and accurately becomes essential to academic achievement. In terms of classroom input, teachers need to cover a range of instructional options, from instruction designed to make content-based input comprehensible by means of various techniques that facilitate comprehension, to instruction designed to make language features more salient. Learners in immersion and content-based classrooms benefit from a broad spectrum of continual opportunities to process input for comprehending subject matter as well as for restructuring their representations of the target language through noticing and awareness activities. In terms of target language production, teachers need again to create a range of opportunities, which vary from content-based tasks designed to promote the use of the target language for academic purposes, to practice activities designed to promote the proceduralization of target language forms that tend otherwise to be avoided, misused, or unnoticed. In terms of classroom interaction, teachers and students need to negotiate language across the curriculum, as teachers exploit a range of interactional techniques that vary from the use of implicit feedback in the form of recasts that scaffold interaction in ways that facilitate students' participation, to feedback in the form of prompts and other signals that push learners beyond their use of recalcitrant interlanguage forms.

Counterbalanced instruction can be adapted across a range of content-based settings defined by different entry points (e.g., early, middle, or late immersion). Dicks (1992) observed that language arts lessons tended to be more experiential for early French immersion students and more analytic for middle and late French immersion students. Harley and Hart (1997), in their comparison of early and late French immersion students in Grade 11, indeed found that second language outcomes were predicted by memory ability in the case of early immersion students and by analytic language ability in the case of late immersion students. In line with the counterbalance hypothesis, Lyster and Mori (in press) suggested that (a) students in late immersion will benefit from the inclusion of more meaning-focused activities that encourage spontaneous production and quick access to unanalyzed language chunks stored as such in long-term memory (Skehan 1998), and (b) students in early immersion will benefit from the inclusion of more form-focused age-appropriate activities, because developing their analytic language ability will prime them for the kind of implicit analysis of naturalistic input in which they need to engage to drive their interlanguage development forward (see Ranta 2002; Skehan 1998).

Genesee (1987) proposed that "continuous growth in the second language will occur only if there are increased demands made on the learners' language system" (p. 59). Counterbalanced instruction increases such demands by pushing learners to shift their attentional focus in a way that then balances their awareness of both form and meaning alike. To avoid overemphasizing language at the expense of content, instructional counterbalance is critical to the integration of more attention to language in immersion and content-based instruction. Day and Shapson (1996) rightly pointed out an important caveat relating to calls for more focus on language in content-based instruction: "Content or subject matter may be seen only as providing the context for learning language and consequently be deemphasized. In addition, surface features of language may be stressed, and the critical role language plays as a medium for learning in all subject areas may be overlooked" (p. 44). Without sacrificing language at the expense of content nor content at the expense of language, counterbalanced instruction emphasizes a flexible and relatively balanced integration of content-based and form-focused instructional options.

3.   Conclusion

With respect to form-focused instructional options, both proactive and reactive approaches need to be counterbalanced in complementary ways within the broader context of language across the curriculum and its associated literacy-based approaches. Proactive form-focused instruction is crucial to classroom learners who would otherwise be required to process the target language exclusively through content and meaning-based activities. In keeping with cognitive theory, proactive form-focused instruction has been characterized throughout this book as (a) noticing and language awareness activities to enable learners to restructure interlanguage representations, and (b) practice activities to enable learners to proceduralize more target-like representations. Reactive form-focused instruction allows learners to put into practice during purposeful interaction the target language knowledge they gain from proactive instructional activities. If teachers were to rely exclusively on reactive approaches, students would soon be discouraged by being pushed in ostensibly random ways to refine their target language output, without the possibility of accessing linguistic support provided systematically through proactive instruction. Contrary to attested "common sense" approaches, whereby teachers avoid at all costs interrupting students during communicative interaction, it appears to be the case, according to current theories of transfer-appropriate learning, that providing feedback "in the heat of the moment" may be the most efficient and effective technique. According to recent classroom intervention studies, teacher prompts designed to push students to retrieve more accurate target forms from their own linguistic resources are particularly effective in meaning-oriented classrooms and have the added benefit of being seamlessly consistent with instructional feedback deemed effective in subject-matter classrooms (McHoul 1990) and in expert-novice tutoring sessions (Lepper et al. 1990). Complementary to the negotiation of form and integral to content-based instruction is negotiation in which teachers provide helpful scaffolding to learners as part of a joint effort shared by both mentor and novice to facilitate the latter's participation as well as the appropriation of target content. In keeping with a socio-cognitive view of second language development, scaffolded interaction with its many opportunities for learners to negotiate language through content serves to fuse content and language, thereby providing instructional coherence across the curriculum in immersion and content-based classrooms.

Content-based and form-focused instructional options need to be counterbalanced in order to provide second language learners with a range of opportunities to process and negotiate language across the curriculum. A case has been made here for counterbalancing these various instructional options, rather than resorting to traditional decontextualized grammar instruction on the one hand, and content instruction with only incidental mention of language on the other. With its inherent pedagogical flexibility, counterbalanced instruction has the requisite propensity for engaging learners with language across the curriculum and thus for mining the full potential of language as a powerful cognitive tool for learning. The counterbalanced approach proposed here provides a tentative framework for systematically addressing the integration of language and content, in the hope that educators in meaning-based classrooms will be better positioned to integrate more focus on language, and that those in traditional language-focused classrooms will be inspired to integrate more content-based instruction as a means of enriching classroom discourse.

References

Aljaafreh, A., & Lantolf, J. (1994). Negative feedback as regulation and second language learning in the zone of proximal development. *The Modern Language Journal, 78*, 465–483.

Allen, P. (1983). A three-level curriculum model for second-language education. *The Canadian Modern Language Review, 40*, 23–43.

Allen, P., Swain, & Harley, B. (1988). Analytic and experiential aspects of core French and immersion classrooms. *Bulletin of the Canadian Association of Applied Linguistics, 10*, 59–68.

Allen, P., Swain, M., Harley, B., & Cummins J. (1990). Aspects of classroom treatment: Toward a more comprehensive view of second language education. In B. Harley, P. Allen, J. Cummins, & M. Swain (Eds.), *The development of second language proficiency* (pp. 57–81). Cambridge, UK: Cambridge University Press.

Allwright, D., & Bailey, K. (1991). *Focus on the language classroom*. New York: Cambridge University Press.

Allwright, R. L. (1975). Problems in the study of the language teacher's treatment of learner error. In M. Burt & H. Dulay (Eds.), *New directions in second language learning, teaching and bilingual education: On TESOL '75* (pp. 96–109). Washington, DC: TESOL.

Allwright, R. L. (1984). Why don't learners learn what teachers teach? The interaction hypothesis. In D. Singleton & D. Little (Eds.), *Language learning in formal and informal contexts* (pp. 3–18). Dublin: IRAAL.

Ammar, A., & Spada, N. (2006). One size fits all? Recasts, prompts and L2 learning. *Studies in Second Language Acquisition, 28*, 543–574.

Anderson, J. R. (1983). *The architecture of cognition*. Cambridge, MA: Harvard University Press.

Anderson, J. R. (1985). *Cognitive psychology and its implications* (2nd ed.). New York: Freeman.

Anderson, J. R., Corbett, A., Koedinger, K. & Pelletier, R. (1995). Cognitive tutors: Lessons learned. *Journal of Learning Sciences, 4*, 167–207.

Arkoudis, S. (2006). Negotiating the rough ground between ESL and mainstream teachers. *International Journal of Bilingual Education and Bilingualism, 9*, 415–433.

Artigal, J. (1991). *The Catalan immersion program: A European point of view*. Norwood, NJ: Ablex.

Artigal, J. (1997). The Catalan immersion program. In K. Johnson & M. Swain (Eds.), *Immersion education: International perspectives* (pp. 133–150). Cambridge, UK: Cambridge University Press.

Arzamendi, J., & Genesee, F. (1998). Reflections on immersion education in the Basque Country. In K. Johnson & M. Swain (Eds.), *Immersion education: International perspectives* (pp. 151–166). Cambridge, UK: Cambridge University Press.

Astley, H., & Hawkins, E. (1985). *Using language.* Cambridge, UK: Cambridge University Press.

Aston, G. (1986). Trouble-shooting in interaction with learners: The more the merrier? *Applied Linguistics, 7,* 128–143.

Auger, J. (2002). French immersion in Montreal: Pedagogical norms and functional competence. In S. Gass, K. Bardovi-Harlig, S. Magnan, & J. Walz (Eds.), *Pedagogical norms for second and foreign language learning and teaching* (pp. 81–101). Amsterdam/Philadelphia: John Benjamins.

August, D., & Hakuta, K. (Eds.). (1997). *Improving schooling for language-minority children: A research agenda.* Washington, DC: National Academy Press.

Austin, J. (1962). *How to do things with words.* Oxford: Oxford University Press.

Bachman, L. (1990). *Fundamental considerations in language testing.* Oxford: Oxford University Press.

Baker, C. (1993). Bilingual education in Wales. In H. Baetens Beardsmore (Ed.), *European models of bilingual education* (pp. 7–29). Clevedon, UK: Multilingual Matters.

Baker, C. (2000). *Foundations of bilingual education and bilingualism* (4th ed.). Clevedon, UK: Multilingual Matters.

Bange, P. (with Carol, R., & Griggs, P.). (2005). *L'apprentissage d'une langue étrangère: cognition et interaction.* Paris: L'Harmattan.

Bardovi-Harlig, K. (2000). *Tense and aspect in second language acquisition: Form, meaning, and use.* Oxford: Blackwell.

Barret, M. (2000). *Diverses fonctions de la référence pronominale dans le discours immersif.* Unpublished M.Ed. monograph, McGill University, Montreal, Canada.

Benton, R. (2001). Balancing tradition and modernity: A natural approach to Mäori language revitalization in a New Zealand secondary school. In D. Christian & F. Genesee (Eds.), *Bilingual education* (pp. 95–108). Alexandria, VA: TESOL.

Bérard, E., & Lavenne, C. (1991). *Grammaire utile du français,* Paris: Hatier.

Bernhardt, E. (Ed.). (1992). *Life in language immersion classrooms.* Clevedon, UK: Multilingual Matters.

Bialystok, E. (1994). Analysis and control in the development of second language proficiency. *Studies in Second Language Acquisition, 16,* 157–168.

Bialystok, E. (2001). *Bilingualism in development: Language, literacy, and cognition.* New York: Cambridge University Press.

Bibeau, G. (1982). *L'éducation bilingue en Amérique du Nord.* Montreal, QC: Guérin.

Björklund, S. (1997). Immersion in Finland in the 1990s: A state of development and expansion. In K. Johnson & M. Swain (Eds.), *Immersion education: International perspectives* (pp. 85–101). Cambridge, UK: Cambridge University Press.

Block, D. (2003). *The social turn in second language acquisition.* Washington, DC: Georgetown University Press.

Bosquart, M. (1998). *Nouvelle grammaire.* Montreal: Guérin.

Bostwick, M. (2001a). Bilingual education of children in Japan: Year four of a partial immersion programme. In M. G. Noguchi & S. Fotos (Eds.), *Studies in Japanese bilingualism* (pp. 272–311). Clevedon, UK: Multilingual Matters.

Bostwick, M. (2001b). English immersion in a Japanese school. In D. Christian & F. Genesee (Eds.), *Bilingual education* (pp. 125–138). Alexandria, VA: TESOL.

Brinton, D., Snow, M., & Wesche, M. (1989). *Content-based second language instruction.* New York: Newbury House.

Braidi, S. (1995). Reconsidering the role of interaction and input in second language acquisition. *Language Learning, 45,* 141–175.

Braidi, S. (2002). Reexamining the role of recasts in native-speaker/nonnative-speaker interactions. *Language Learning, 52,* 1–42.

Brock, C., Crookes, G., Day, R., & Long, M. (1986). The differential effects of corrective feedback in native speaker-nonnative speaker conversation. In R. Day (Ed.), *Talking to learn* (pp. 229–236). Rowley, MA: Newbury House.

Broner, M., & Tarone, E. (2002). Is it fun? Language play in a 5th grade Spanish immersion class. *The Canadian Modern Language Review, 58,* 526–554.

Bruner, J. (1967). *Toward a theory of instruction.* Cambridge, MA: Harvard University Press.

Bruner, J. (1971). *The relevance of education.* New York: Norton.

Bruner, J. (1977). *The process of education.* [First published in 1960]. Cambridge, MA: Harvard University Press.

Bruner, J. (1986). *Actual minds, possible worlds.* Cambridge, MA: Harvard University Press.

Burger, S., & Chrétien, S. (2001). The development of oral production in content-based second language courses at the University of Ottawa. *The Canadian Modern Language Review, 58,* 84–102.

Burger, S., Wesche, M., & Migneron, M. (1997). "Late, late immersion": Discipline-based second language teaching at the University of Ottawa. In K. Johnson & M. Swain (Eds.), *Immersion education: International perspectives* (pp. 65–84). Cambridge, UK: Cambridge University Press.

Burmeister, P., & Daniel, A. (2002). How effective is late partial immersion? Some findings of a secondary school program in Germany. In P. Burmeister, T. Piske, & A. Rohde (Eds.), *An integrated view of language development: Papers in honor of Henning Wode* (pp. 499–516). Trier, Germany: Wissenschaftlicher Verlag Trier.

Bygate, M. (1999). Task as context for the framing, reframing and unframing of language. *System, 27,* 33–48.

Bygate, M., Skehan, P., & Swain, M. (Eds.). (2001). *Researching pedagogic tasks: Second language learning, teaching and testing.* Harlow, UK: Pearson Education.

CAIT (1995). *Introducing English language arts in early French immersion.* Ottawa: ON: Canadian Association of Immersion Teachers.

Caldas, S. (2006). *Raising bilingual-biliterate children in monolingual cultures.* Clevedon, UK: Multilingual Matters.

Calvé, P. (1986). L'immersion au secondaire: bilan et perspectives. *CONTACT, 5* (3), 21–28.

Cameron, L. (2001). *Teaching languages to young learners.* Cambridge, UK: Cambridge University Press.

Canale, M. (1983). From communicative competence to communicative language pedagogy. In J. C. Richards & R. W. Schmidt (Eds.), *Language and communication* (pp. 2–27). London: Longman.

Canale, M., & Swain, M. (1980). Theoretical bases of communicative approaches to second language teaching and testing. *Applied Linguistics, 1*, 1–47.

Carpenter, H., Jeon, K. S., MacGregor, D., & Mackey, A. (2006). Learners' interpretations of recasts. *Studies in Second Language Acquisition, 28*, 209–236.

Carroll, S. (1989). Second-language acquisition and the computational paradigm. *Language Learning, 39*, 535–594.

Carroll, S. (1999). Input and SLA: Adults' sensitivity to different sorts of cues to French gender. *Language Learning, 49*, 37–92.

Carroll, S., & Swain, M. (1993). Explicit and implicit negative feedback: An empirical study of the learning of linguistic generalizations. *Studies in Second Language Acquisition, 15*, 357–386.

Cary, A. (2001). Affiliation, not assimilation: Resident Koreans and ethnic education. In M. G. Noguchi & S. Fotos (Eds.), *Studies in Japanese bilingualism* (pp. 68–97). Clevedon, UK: Multilingual Matters.

Cathcart, R., & Olsen, J. (1976). Teachers' and students' preferences for correction of classroom conversation errors. In J. F. Fanselow & R. H. Crymes (Eds.), *On TESOL '76* (pp. 41–53). Washington, DC: TESOL.

Cazabon, B., & Size-Cazabon, J. (1987). Who can succeed in learning French? Is it for everyone? *CONTACT, 6* (3), 3–8.

Cenoz, J. (1998). Multilingual education in the Basque Country. In J. Cenoz & F. Genesee (Eds.), *Beyond bilingualism: Multilingualism and multilingual education* (pp. 175–191). Clevedon, UK: Multilingual Matters.

Chaudron, C. (1977). A descriptive model of discourse in the corrective treatment of learners' errors. *Language Learning, 27*, 29–46.

Chaudron, C. (1986). Teachers' priorities in correcting learners' errors in French immersion classes. In R. Day (Ed.), *Talking to learn* (pp. 64–84). Rowley, MA: Newbury House.

Chaudron, C. (1988). *Second language classrooms.* New York: Cambridge University Press.

Chomsky, N. (1965). *Aspects of the theory of syntax.* Cambridge, MA: MIT Press.

Christian, D., & Genesee, F. (Eds.). (2001). *Bilingual education.* Alexandra, VA: TESOL.

Clark, S. (1995). The generation effect and the modeling of associations in memory. *Memory & Cognition, 23*, 442–455.

Clipperton, R. (1994). Explicit vocabulary instruction in French immersion. *The Canadian Modern Language Review, 50*, 737–749.

Cloud, N., Genesee, F., & Hamayan, E. (2000). *Dual language instruction: A handbook for enriched education.* Boston: Heinle & Heinle.

Collins, J. (1982). Discourse style, classroom interaction and differential treatment. *Journal of Reading Behavior, 14*, 429–437.

Collins, L. (2002). The roles of L2 influence and lexical aspect in the acquisition of temporal morphology. *Language Learning, 52*, 43–94.

Cook, V. (2001). Using the first language in the classroom. *The Canadian Modern Language Review, 57*, 402–423.

Corder, S. P. (1967). The significance of learners' errors. *International Review of Applied Linguistics, 4,* 161–170.

Corson, D. (1999). Language across the curriculum. In B. Spolsky (Ed.), *Concise encyclopedia of educational linguistics* (pp. 323–325). Oxford, UK: Pergamon.

Creese, A. (2002). The discursive construction of power in teacher partnerships: Language and subject specialists in mainstream schools. *TESOL Quarterly, 36,* 597–616.

Creese, A. (2006). Supporting talk? Partnership teachers in classroom interaction. *International Journal of Bilingual Education and Bilingualism, 9,* 434–453.

Cummins, J. (1981). The role of primary language development in promoting educational success for language minority students. In *Schooling and language minority students: A theoretical framework* (pp. 3–49). Los Angeles: California State University.

Cummins, J. (1986). Empowering minority students: A framework for intervention. *Harvard Educational Review, 56,* 18–36.

Cummins, J. (1989) *Empowering minority students.* Sacramento, CA: California Association for Bilingual Education.

Cummins, J. (1994). Knowledge, power, and identity in teaching English as a second language. In F. Genesee (Ed.), *Educating second language children* (pp. 33–58). New York: Cambridge University Press.

Cummins, J. (2000). *Language, power, and pedagogy: Bilingual children in the crossfire.* Clevedon, UK: Multilingual Matters.

Cummins, J., & Swain, M. (1986). *Bilingualism in education.* London: Longman.

Dalton-Puffer, C. (2006). Questions in CLIL classrooms: Strategic questioning to encourage speaking. In A. Martinez-Flor & E. Usó (Eds.), *Current trends in the development of the four skills within a communicative framework* (pp. 187–213). Berlin: Mouton de Gruyter.

Day, E. & Shapson, S. (1991). Integrating formal and functional approaches to language teaching in French immersion: An experimental study. *Language Learning, 41,* 25–58.

Day, E., & Shapson, S. (1996). *Studies in immersion education.* Clevedon, UK: Multilingual Matters.

de Bot, K. (1996). The psycholinguistics of the output hypothesis. *Language Learning, 46.* 529–555.

de Bot, K. (2000). Psycholinguistics in applied linguistics: Trends and perspectives. *Annual Review of Applied Linguistics, 20,* 224–237.

DeKeyser, R. (1998). Beyond focus on form: Cognitive perspectives on learning and practicing second language grammar. In C. Doughty & J. Williams (Eds.), *Focus on form in classroom second language acquisition* (pp. 42–63). Cambridge, UK: Cambridge University Press.

DeKeyser, R. (2001). Automaticity and automatization. In P. Robinson (Ed.), *Cognition and second language instruction* (pp. 125–51). Cambridge, UK: Cambridge University Press.

DeKeyser, R. (Ed.). (2007). *Practice in a second language: Perspectives from applied linguistics and cognitive psychology.* Cambridge, UK: Cambridge University Press.

De Pietro, J.-F., Matthey, M., & Py, B. (1989). Acquisition et contrat didactique: les séquences potentiellement acquisitionnelles dans la conversation exolingue. In D. Weil & H. Fugier (Eds.), *Actes du Troisième Colloque Régional de Linguistique* (pp. 99–124). Strasbourg: Université des sciences humaines et Université Louis Pasteur.

deWinstanley, P. A., & Bjork, E. L. (2004). Processing strategies and the generation effect: Implications for making a better reader. *Memory & Cognition, 32*, 945–955.

DiCamilla, F. J. & Anton, M. (1997). Repetition in the collaborative discourse of L2 learners: A Vygotskian perspective. *The Canadian Modern Language Review, 43*, 609–633.

Dicks, J. (1992). Analytic and experiential features of three French immersion programs: Early, middle, and late. *The Canadian Modern Language Review, 49*, 37–59.

Donaldson, M. (1978). *Children's minds*. New York: Norton.

Donato, R. (1994). Collective scaffolding in second language learning. In J. Lantolf & G. Appel (Eds.), *Vygotskian approaches to second language research* (pp. 33–56). Norwood, NJ: Ablex.

Doughty, C. (1991). Second language instruction does make a difference: Evidence from an empirical study of SL relativization. *Studies in Second Language Acquisition, 13*, 431–469.

Doughty, C. (1994). Fine-tuning of feedback by competent speakers to language learners. In J. Alatis (Ed.), *Georgetown University Round Table 1993: Strategic interaction and language acquisition* (pp. 96–108). Washington, DC: Georgetown University Press.

Doughty, C. (2001). Cognitive underpinnings of focus on form. In P. Robinson (Ed.), *Cognition and second language instruction* (pp. 206–257). New York: Cambridge University Press.

Doughty, C., & Varela, E. (1998). Communicative focus on form. In C. Doughty & J. Williams (Eds.), *Focus on form in classroom second language acquisition* (pp. 114–138). Cambridge, UK: Cambridge University Press.

Doughty, C., & Williams, J. (1998). Pedagogical choices in focus on form. In C. Doughty & J. Williams (Eds.), *Focus on form in classroom second language acquisition* (pp. 197–261). Cambridge, UK: Cambridge University Press.

Dubin, F., & Olshtain, E. (1986). *Course design: Developing programs and materials for language learning*. Cambridge: Cambridge University Press.

Duff, P. (1995). An ethnography of communication in immersion classrooms in Hungary. *TESOL Quarterly, 29*, 505–537.

Duff, P. (1997). Immersion in Hungary: An EFL experiment. In K. Johnson & M. Swain (Eds.), *Immersion education: International perspectives* (pp. 19–43). Cambridge, UK: Cambridge University Press.

Early, M. (2001). Language and content in social practice: A case study. *The Canadian Modern Language Review, 58*, 156–179.

Echevarria, J., & Graves, A. (1998). *Sheltered content instruction*. Boston: Allyn & Bacon.

Ellis, R. (1986). *Understanding second language acquisition*. Oxford: Oxford University Press.

Ellis, R. (2000). Task-based research and language pedagogy. *Language Teaching Research, 4*, 193–220.

Ellis, R. (2001). Investigating form-focused instruction. *Language Learning, 51* (Suppl. 1), 1–46.

Ellis, R. (2002). The place of grammar instruction in the second/foreign curriculum. In E. Hinkel & S. Fotos (Eds.), *New perspectives on grammar teaching in second language classrooms* (pp. 17–34). Mahwah, NJ: Lawrence Erlbaum.

Ellis, R. (2003). *Task-based language learning and teaching*. Oxford: Oxford University Press.

Ellis, R., Basturkmen, H., & Loewen, S. (2001). Learner uptake in communicative ESL lessons. *Language Learning, 51*, 281–318.

Ellis, R., Loewen, S., & Erlam, R. (2006). Implicit and explicit corrective feedback and the acquisition of L2 grammar. *Studies in Second Language Acquisition, 28*, 339–368.

Ellis, R., & Sheen, Y. (2006). Re-examining the role of recasts in L2 acquisition. *Studies in Second Language Acquisition, 28*, 575–600.

Fazio, L., & Lyster, R. (1998). Immersion and submersion classrooms: A comparison of instructional practices in language arts. *Journal of Multilingual and Multicultural Development, 19*, 303–317.

Foster, P. (1998). A classroom perspective on the negotiation of meaning. *Applied Linguistics, 19*, 1–23.

Foster, P., & Ohta, A. (2005). Negotiation for meaning and peer assistance in second language classrooms. *Applied Linguistics, 26*, 402–430.

Gass, S. (1988). Integrating research areas: A framework for second language studies. *Applied Linguistics, 9*, 198–217.

Gass, S. (1997). *Input, interaction, and the second language learner.* Mahwah, NJ: Lawrence Erlbaum.

Gass, S., & Varonis, E. (1994). Input, interaction, and second language production. *Studies in Second Language Acquisition, 16*, 283–302.

Genesee, F. (1987). *Learning through two languages: Studies of immersion and bilingual children.* Cambridge, MA: Newbury House.

Genesee, F. (1991). Second language learning in school settings: Lessons from immersion. In A. Reynolds (Ed.), *Bilingualism, multiculturalism, and second language learning* (pp. 183–202). Hillsdale, NJ: Lawrence Erlbaum.

Genesee, F. (1992). Second/foreign language immersion and at-risk English-speaking children. *Foreign Language Annals, 25*, 199–213.

Genesee, F. (1994a). *Integrating language and content: Lessons from immersion.* [Educational Practice Report No. 11]. Santa Cruz, CA: National Center for Research on Cultural Diversity and Second Language Learning.

Genesee, F. (1994b). Some holes in whole language. *TESOL Matters, 4* (3), p. 3.

Genesee, F. (1998). A case study of multilingual education in Canada. In J. Cenoz & F. Genesee (Eds.), *Beyond bilingualism: Multilingualism and multilingual education* (pp. 243–58). Clevedon, UK: Multilingual Matters.

Genesee, F. (2004). What do we know about bilingual education for majority language students? In T. K. Bhatia & W. Ritchie (Eds.), *Handbook of bilingualism and multiculturalism* (pp. 547–576). Malden, MA: Blackwell.

Genesee, F. (2006). *The suitability of French immersion for students who are at risk: A review of research evidence.* Ottawa, ON: Canadian Parents for French.

Genesee, F., & Gándara, P. (1999). Bilingual education programs: A cross-national perspective. *Journal of Social Issues, 55*, 665–685.

Genesee, F., & Lambert, W. (1983). Trilingual education for majority-language children. *Child Development, 54*, 105–114.

Germain, C. (1993). *Évolution de l'enseignement des langues : 5000 ans d'histoire.* Paris: CLE International.

Gibbons, P. (1998). Classroom talk and the learning of new registers in a second language. *Language and Education, 12*, 99–118.

Gibbons, P. (2003). Mediating language learning: Teacher interactions with ESL students in a content-based classroom. *TESOL Quarterly, 37*, 247–273.

Giroux, H. (1992). *Border crossings: Cultural workers and the politics of education*. New York: Routledge.

Gumperz, J. (1972). Sociolinguistics and communication in small groups. In J. Pride & J. Holmes (Eds.), *Sociolinguistics: Selected readings* (pp. 203–224). Harmondsworthe, UK: Penguin.

Hall, K. (1993). Process writing in French immersion. *The Canadian Modern Language Review, 49*, 255–274.

Han, Z. (2002). A study of the impact of recasts on tense consistency in L2 output. *TESOL Quarterly, 36*, 542–572.

Haneda, M. (2005). Functions of triadic dialogue in the classroom: Examples for L2 research. *The Canadian Modern Language Review, 62*, 313–333.

Handscombe, J. (1990). The complementary roles of researchers and practitioners in second language education. In B. Harley, P. Allen, J. Cummins & M. Swain (Eds.), *The development of second language proficiency* (pp. 181–186). Cambridge, UK: Cambridge University Press.

Harley, B. (1979). French gender 'rules' in the speech of English-dominant, French-dominant, and monolingual French-speaking children. *Working Papers in Bilingualism, 19*, 129–156.

Harley, B. (1980). Interlanguage units and their relations. *Interlanguage Studies Bulletin, 5*, 3–30.

Harley, B. (1984). How good is their French? *Language and Society, 12* (Winter), 55–60.

Harley, B. (1986). *Age in second language acquisition*. Clevedon, UK: Multilingual Matters.

Harley, B. (1989). Functional grammar in French immersion: A classroom experiment. *Applied Linguistics, 10*, 331–359.

Harley, B. (1992). Patterns of second language development in French immersion. *Journal of French Language Studies, 2*, 159–183.

Harley, B. (1993). Instructional strategies and SLA in early French immersion. *Studies in Second Language Acquisition, 15*, 245–259.

Harley, B. (1994). Appealing to consciousness in the L2 classroom. *AILA Review, 11*, 57–68.

Harley, B. (1998) The role of form-focused tasks in promoting child L2 acquisition. In C. Doughty & J. Williams (Eds.), *Focus on form in classroom second language acquisition* (pp. 156–174). Cambridge, UK: Cambridge University Press.

Harley, B., Allen, P., Cummins, J., & Swain, M. (Eds.). (1987). *Development of bilingual proficiency. Final report. Volume II: Classroom treatment*. Toronto, ON: Modern Language Centre, OISE/UT.

Harley, B., Cummins, J., Swain, M., & Allen, P. (1990). The nature of language proficiency. In B. Harley, P. Allen, J. Cummins & M. Swain (Eds.), *The development of second language proficiency* (pp. 7–25). Cambridge, UK: Cambridge University Press.

Harley, B., & Hart, D. (1997). Language aptitude and second language proficiency in classroom learners of different starting ages. *Studies in Second Language Acquisition, 19*, 379–400.

Harley, B., Howard, J., & Roberge, B. (1996). Teaching vocabulary: An exploratory study of direct techniques. *The Canadian Modern Language Review, 53,* 281–304.

Harley, B. & King, M. (1989). Verb lexis in the written compositions of young L2 learners. *Studies in Second Language Acquisition, 11,* 415–439.

Harley, B. & Swain, M. (1984). The interlanguage of immersion students and its implications for second language teaching. In A. Davies, C. Criper & A. Howatt (Eds.), *Interlanguage* (pp. 291–311). Edinburgh: Edinburgh University Press.

Havranek, G. (2002). When is corrective feedback most likely to succeed? *International Journal of Educational Research, 37,* 255–270.

Havranek, G., & Cesnik, H. (2001). Factors affecting the success of corrective feedback. *EUROSLA Yearbook, 1,* 99–122.

Hawkins, E. (1984). *Awareness of language: An introduction.* Cambridge, UK: Cambridge University Press.

Heller, M., Barker, G., & Lévy, L. (1989). *Projets de recherche et d'apprentissage coopératif: l'annonce publicitaire.* Toronto, ON: Centre de recherches en éducation franco-ontarienne, OISE/UT.

Hendrickson, J. (1978). Error correction in foreign language teaching: Recent theory, research, and practice. *The Modern Language Journal, 62,* 387–398.

Hickey, T. (2001). Mixing beginners and native speakers in minority language immersion: Who is immersing whom? *The Canadian Modern Language Review, 57,* 443–474.

Hickman, J. (1992). Whole language and literature in a French immersion elementary school. In E. Bernhardt (Ed.), *Life in language immersion classrooms* (pp. 84–96). Clevedon, UK: Multilingual Matters.

Hobbs, J., & Nasso-Maselli, M. (2005). *Elementary programs study.* St. Lambert, QC: Riverside School Board.

Howard, E., Christian, D., & Genesee, F. (2004). *The development of bilingualism and biliteracy from grade 3 to 5: A summary of findings from the CAL/CREDE study of two-way immersion education.* Santa Cruz, CA: Center for Research on Education, Diversity & Excellence.

Hullen, J. & Lentz, F. (1991). Pour une rentabilisation des pratiques pédagogiques en immersion. *Études de linguistique appliquée, 82,* 63–76.

Hulstijn, J. (1990). A comparison between the information-processing and the analysis/control approaches to language learning. *Applied Linguistics, 11,* 30–45.

Hulstijn, J. (2003). Incidental and intentional learning. In C. Doughty & M. Long (Eds.), *Handbook of second language acquisition* (pp. 349–381). Oxford: Blackwell.

Hymes, D. (1971). Competence and performance in linguistic theory. In R. Huxley & E. Ingram (Eds.), *Language acquisition: Models and methods* (pp. 3–28). London: Academic Press.

Ishida, M. (2004). Effects of recasts on the acquisition of the aspectual form *-te i-(ru)* by learners of Japanese as a foreign language. *Language Learning, 54,* 311–394.

Iwashita, N. (2001). The effect of learner proficiency on interactional moves and modified output in nonnative-nonnative interaction in Japanese as a foreign language. *System, 29,* 267–287.

Izquierdo, J. (in progress). *Computer-mediated focus on form and the acquisition of the tense-aspect system by L2 learners of French.* Unpublished doctoral dissertation, McGill University, Montreal, Canada.

Jacob, R. & Laurin, J. (1994). *Ma grammaire.* Montreal, QC: Les Éditions françaises.

Jacobs, K. A., & Cross, A. E. (2001). The seventh generation of Kahnawà:ke: Phoenix or dinosaur. In D. Christian & F. Genesee (Eds.), *Bilingual education* (pp. 109–121). Alexandria, VA: TESOL.

Jiang, N. (2000). Lexical representation and development in a second language. *Applied Linguistics, 21,* 47–77.

Johnson, K. (1997). The Hong Kong education system: Late immersion under stress. In K. Johnson & M. Swain (Eds.), *Immersion education: International perspectives* (pp. 171–189). Cambridge, UK: Cambridge University Press.

Johnson, K., & Swain, M. (Eds.). (1997). *Immersion education: International perspectives.* Cambridge, UK: Cambridge University Press.

Johnson, R. (1996). *Language teaching and skill learning.* Oxford: Blackwell.

Karmiloff-Smith, A. (1979). *A functional approach to child language.* Cambridge, UK: Cambridge University Press.

Kasper, G. (1985). Repair in foreign language learning. *Studies in Second Language Acquisition, 7,* 200–215.

Kasper, G. (2001). Classroom research on interlanguage pragmatics. In K. Rose & G. Kasper (Eds.), *Pragmatics in language teaching* (pp. 33–60). New York: Cambridge University Press.

Kleifgen, J., & Saville-Troike, M. (1992). Achieving coherence in multilingual interaction. *Discourse Processes, 15,* 183–206.

Klein, W. (1986). *Second language acquisition.* Cambridge, UK: Cambridge University Press.

Kohn, A. (1999). *The schools our children deserve.* New York: Houghton Mifflin.

Kowal, M. & Swain, M. (1994). Using collaborative language production tasks to promote students' language awareness. *Language Awareness, 3,* 73–93.

Kowal, M., & Swain, M. (1997). From semantic to syntactic processing: How can we promote metalinguistic awareness in the French immersion classroom? In R. K. Johnson & M. Swain (Eds.), *Immersion education: International perspectives* (pp. 284–309). Cambridge, UK: Cambridge University Press.

Krashen, S. (1982). *Principles and practice in second language acquisition.* New York: Pergamon.

Krashen, S. (1985). *The input hypothesis: Issues and implications.* London: Longman.

Krashen, S. (1984). Immersion: why it works and what it has taught us. *Language and Society, 12,* 61–68.

Krashen, S. (1994). The input hypothesis and its rivals. In N. Ellis (Ed.), *Implicit and explicit learning of languages* (pp. 45–77). London: Academic Press.

Krashen, S. (1998). Comprehensible output? *System, 26,* 175–182.

Lambert, W., & Tucker, R. (1972). *Bilingual education of children: The St. Lambert experiment.* Rowley, MA: Newbury House.

Lamont, D., Penner, W., Blower, T., Mosychuk, H., & Jones, J. (1978). Evaluation of the second year of a bilingual (English-Ukrainian) program. *The Canadian Modern Language Review, 34,* 175–185.

Lapkin, S., Andrew, C., Harley, B., Swain, M., & Kamin, J. (1981). The immersion centre and the dual-track school: A study of the relationship between school environment and achievement in a French immersion program. *Canadian Journal of Education, 6,* 68–90.

Lapkin, S. & Swain, M. (1996). Vocabulary teaching in a grade 8 French immersion classroom: A descriptive study. *The Canadian Modern Language Review, 53,* 242–256.

Laplante, B. (1993). Stratégies pédagogiques et enseignement des sciences en immersion française: le cas d'une enseignante. *The Canadian Modern Language Review, 49,* 567–588.

Laplante, B. (1997). Teachers' beliefs and instructional strategies in science: Pushing analysis further. *Science Education, 81,* 277–294.

Laufer, B. (2003). Vocabulary acquisition in a second language: Do learners really acquire most vocabulary by reading? Some empirical evidence. *The Canadian Modern Language Review, 59,* 567–588.

Laufer, B. (2006). Comparing focus on form and focus on forms in second language vocabulary learning. *The Canadian Modern Language Review, 63,* 149–166.

Lee, J. (2006). *Corrective feedback and learner uptake in English immersion classrooms in Korea.* Unpublished master's thesis, International Graduate School of English, Seoul, Korea.

Leeman, J. (2003). Recasts and second language development: Beyond negative evidence. *Studies in Second Language Acquisition, 25,* 37–63.

Lemke, J. (1990). *Talking science: Language, learning, and values.* Norwood, NJ: Ablex.

Leow, R. (2007). Input in the L2 classroom: An attentional perspective on receptive practice. In R. DeKeyser (Ed.), *Practicing for second language use: Perspectives from applied linguistics and cognitive psychology* (pp. 21–50). Cambridge, UK: Cambridge University Press.

Lepper, M., Aspinwall, L., Mumme, D., & Chabay, R. (1990). Self-perception and social-perception processes in tutoring: Subtle social control strategies of expert tutors. In J. Olson & M. Zanna (Eds.), *Self-inference processes: The Ontario Symposium, volume 6* (pp. 217–237). Hillsdale, NJ: Lawrence Erlbaum.

Levinson, S. (1983). *Pragmatics.* Cambridge, UK: Cambridge University Press.

Lightbown, P. M. (1985). Great expectations: Second language acquisition research and classroom teaching. *Applied Linguistics, 6,* 173–189.

Lightbown, P. M. (1992). Can they do it themselves? A comprehension-based ESL course for young children. In R. Courchêne, J. Glidden, J. St. John, & C. Thérien (Eds.), *Comprehension-based second language teaching* (pp. 353–370). Ottawa, ON: University of Ottawa Press.

Lightbown, P. M. (1991). What have we here? Some observations on the influence of instruction on L2 learning. In R. Phillipson, E. Kellerman, L. Selinker, M. Sharwood Smith & M. Swain (Eds.), *Foreign/second language pedagogy research* (pp. 197–212). Clevedon, UK: Multilingual Matters.

Lightbown, P. M. (1998). The importance of timing in focus on form. In C. Doughty & J. Williams (eds.), *Focus on form in classroom second language acquisition* (pp. 177–196). Cambridge, UK: Cambridge University Press.

Lightbown, P. M. (2000). Classroom SLA research and second language teaching. *Applied Linguistics, 21,* 431–462.

Lightbown, P. M., Halter, R., White, J., & Horst, M. (2002). Comprehension- based learning: The limits of 'Do it yourself'. *The Canadian Modern Language Review, 58*, 427–464.

Lightbown, P. M., & Spada, N. (1990). Focus on form and corrective feedback in communicative language teaching: Effects on second language learning. *Studies in Second Language Acquisition, 12*, 429–448.

Lightbown, P. M., & Spada, N. (2006). *How languages are learned* (3rd ed.). Oxford: Oxford University Press.

Lim, S. E., Gan, L., & Sharpe, P. (1997). Immersion in Singapore preschools. In K. Johnson & M. Swain (Eds.), *Immersion education: International perspectives* (pp. 190–209). Cambridge, UK: Cambridge University Press.

Lin, Y.-H., & Hedgcock, J. (1996). Negative feedback incorporation among high-proficiency and low-proficiency Chinese-speaking learners of Spanish. *Language Learning, 46*, 567–611.

Lindholm-Leary, K. (2001). *Dual language education.* Clevedon, UK: Multilingual Matters.

Lochtman, K. (2002). Oral corrective feedback in the foreign language classroom: How it affects interaction in analytic foreign language teaching. *International Journal of Educational Research, 37*, 271–283.

Lochtman, K. (2005). Negative feedback and learner uptake in analytic foreign language teaching. In A. Housen & M. Pierrard (Eds.), *Investigations in instructed second language acquisition* (pp. 333–352). Berlin/New York: Mouton de Gruyter.

Loewen, S. (2005). Incidental focus on form and second language learning. *Studies in Second Language Acquisition, 27*, 361–386.

Loewen, S., & Philp, J. (2006). Recasts in the adult English L2 classroom: Characteristics, explicitness, and effectiveness. *The Modern Language Journal, 90*, 536–555.

Logan, G. (1988). Toward an instance theory of automatization. *Psychological Review, 95*, 492–527.

Long, M. (1977). Teacher feedback on learner error: Mapping cognitions. In H. D. Brown, C. A. Yorio, & R. H. Crymes (Eds.), *On TESOL '77* (pp. 278–293). Washington, DC: TESOL.

Long, M. (1983). Native speaker/non-native speaker conversation and the negotiation of comprehensible input. *Applied Linguistics, 4*, 126–141.

Long, M. (1991). Focus on form: A design feature in language teaching methodology. In K. de Bot, R. Ginsberg, & C. Kramsch (Eds.), *Foreign language research in cross-cultural perspective* (pp. 39–52). Amsterdam: John Benjamins.

Long, M. (1996). The role of the linguistic environment in second language acquisition. In W. C. Ritchie & T. K. Bhatia (Eds.), *Handbook of second language acquisition* (pp. 413–468). San Diego, CA: Academic Press.

Long, M. (2007). *Problems in SLA.* Mahwah, NJ: Lawrence Erlbaum.

Long, M., & Robinson, P. (1998). Focus on form: Theory, research, and practice. In C. Doughty & J. Williams (Eds.), *Focus on form in classroom second language acquisition* (pp. 15–41). Cambridge, UK: Cambridge University Press.

Loschky, L., & Bley-Vroman, R. (1993). Grammar and task-based methodology. In G. Crookes & S. Gass (Eds.), *Tasks and language learning: Integrating theory and practice* (pp. 123–167). Clevedon, UK: Multilingual Matters.

Lyster, R. (1987). Speaking immersion. *The Canadian Modern Language Review, 43,* 701–717.

Lyster, R. (1993). *The effect of functional-analytic teaching on aspects of sociolinguistic competence: An experimental study in French immersion classrooms at the Grade 8 level.* Unpublished doctoral dissertation, University of Toronto, Canada.

Lyster, R. (1994a). The effect of functional-analytic teaching on aspects of French immersion students' sociolinguistic competence. *Applied Linguistics, 15,* 263–287.

Lyster, R. (1994b). La négociation de la forme: stratégie analytique en classe d'immersion. *The Canadian Modern Language Review, 50,* 446–465.

Lyster, R. (1998a). Recasts, repetition, and ambiguity in L2 classroom discourse. *Studies in Second Language Acquisition, 20,* 51–81.

Lyster, R. (1998b). Negotiation of form, recasts, and explicit correction in relation to error types and learner repair in immersion classrooms. *Language Learning, 48,* 183–218.

Lyster, R. (1998c). Immersion pedagogy and implications for language teaching. In J. Cenoz & F. Genesee (Eds.), *Beyond bilingualism: Multilingualism and multilingual education* (pp. 64–95). Clevedon, UK: Multilingual Matters.

Lyster, R. (1998d). Form in immersion classroom discourse: In or out of focus? *Canadian Journal of Applied Linguistics, 1,* 53–82.

Lyster, R. (1998e). Diffusing dichotomies: Using the multidimensional curriculum model for developing analytic teaching materials in immersion. In S. Lapkin (Ed.) *French second language education in Canada: Empirical studies* (pp. 195–217). Toronto, ON: University of Toronto Press.

Lyster, R. (2002a). Negotiation in immersion teacher-student interaction. *International Journal of Educational Research, 37,* 237–253.

Lyster, R. (2002b). The importance of differentiating negotiation of form and meaning in classroom interaction. In P. Burmeister, T. Piske, & A. Rohde (Eds.), *An integrated view of language development: Papers in honor of Henning Wode* (pp. 381–397). Trier, Germany: Wissenschaftlicher Verlag Trier.

Lyster, R. (2004a). Differential effects of prompts and recasts in form-focused instruction. *Studies in Second Language Acquisition, 26,* 399–432.

Lyster, R. (2004b). Research on form-focused instruction in immersion classrooms: Implications for theory and practice. *Journal of French Language Studies, 14,* 321–341.

Lyster, R. (2006). Predictability in French gender attribution: A corpus analysis. *Journal of French Language Studies, 16,* 69–92.

Lyster, R., & Mori, H. (2006). Interactional feedback and instructional counterbalance. *Studies in Second Language Acquisition, 28,* 269–300.

Lyster, R., & Mori, H. (in press). Instructional counterbalance in immersion pedagogy. In T. Fortune & D. Tedick (Eds.), *Pathways to bilingualism and multilingualism: Evolving perspectives on immersion education.* Clevedon, UK: Multilingual Matters.

Lyster, R., & Ranta, L. (1997). Corrective feedback and learner uptake: Negotiation of form in communicative classrooms. *Studies in Second Language Acquisition, 19,* 37–66.

Lyster, R., & Rebuffot, J. (2002). Acquisition des pronoms d'allocution en classe de français immersif. *Acquisition et Interaction en Langue Étrangère, 17,* 51–71.

MacFarlane, A. (2001). Are brief contact experiences and classroom language learning complementary? *The Canadian Modern Language Review, 58,* 64–83.

MacIntyre, P., Baker, S., Clément, R., & Donovan, L. (2003). Talking in order learn: Willingness to communicate and intensive language programs. *The Canadian Modern Language Review, 59*, 589–607.

Mackey, A. (1999). Input, interaction, and second language development. *Studies in Second Language Acquisition, 21*, 557–588.

Mackey A., Gass S., & McDonough, K. (2000). How do learners perceive interactional feedback? *Studies in Second Language Acquisition, 22*, 471–497.

Mackey, A., Oliver, R., & Leeman, J. (2003). Interactional input and the incorporation of feedback: An exploration of NS-NNS and NNS-NNS adult and child dyads. *Language Learning, 53*, 35–66.

Mackey, A., & Philp, J. (1998). Conversational interaction and second language development: Recasts, responses, and red herrings? *The Modern Language Journal, 82*, 338–356.

Marsh, D., Maljers, A., & Hartiala, A.-K. (Eds.). (2001). *Profiling European CLIL classrooms*. Jyväskylä, Finland: University of Jyväskylä.

Marsh, H., & Hau, K., & Kong, C. (2000). Late immersion and language of instruction in Hong Kong high schools: Achievement growth in language and nonlanguage subjects. *Harvard Educational Review, 70*, 302–346.

McCormick, D., & Donato, R. (2000). Teacher questions as scaffolded assistance in an ESL classroom. In J. K. Hall and L. Verplaetse (Eds.), *Second and foreign language learning through classroom interaction* (pp. 183–201). Mahwah, NJ: Lawrence Erlbaum.

McDonough, K. (2005). Identifying the impact of negative feedback and learners' responses on ESL question development. *Studies in Second Language Acquisition, 27*, 79–103.

McDonough, K. (2006). Interaction and syntactic priming: English L2 speakers' production of dative constructions. *Studies in Second Language Acquisition, 28*, 179–208.

McDonough, K., & Mackey, A. (2000). Communicative tasks, conversational interaction and linguistic form: An empirical study of Thai. *Foreign Language Annals, 33*, 82–91.

McHoul, A. (1990). The organization of repair in classroom talk. *Language in Society, 19*, 349–377.

McLaughlin, B. (1987). *Theories of second-language learning*. London: Edward Arnold.

McLaughlin, B. (1990). Restructuring. *Applied Linguistics, 11*, 113–128.

McLaughlin, B., & Heredia, R. (1996). Information-processing approaches to research on second language acquisition and use. In W.C. Ritchie & T.K. Bhatia (Eds.), *Handbook of second language acquisition* (pp. 213–228). San Diego, CA: Academic Press.

Mendez, C. (1992). How many Wednesdays? A portrait of immersion teaching through reflection. In E. Bernhardt (Ed.), *Life in language immersion classrooms* (pp. 45–63). Clevedon, UK: Multilingual Matters.

Mercer, N. (1999). Classroom language. In B. Spolsky (Ed.), *Concise encyclopedia of educational linguistics* (pp. 315–319). Oxford, UK: Pergamon.

Met, M. (1994). Teaching content through a second language. In F. Genesee (Ed.), *Educating second language children* (pp. 159–182). New York: Cambridge University Press.

Met, M. (1998). Curriculum decision-making in content-based language teaching. In J. Cenoz & F. Genesee (Eds.), *Beyond bilingualism: Multilingualism and multilingual education* (pp. 35–63). Clevedon, UK: Multilingual Matters.

Met, M., & Lorenz, E. (1997). Lessons from U.S. immersion programs: Two decades of experience. In K. Johnson & M. Swain (Eds.), *Immersion education: International perspectives* (pp. 243–264). Cambridge, UK: Cambridge University Press

Mey, J. (1993). *Pragmatics: An introduction.* Oxford: Blackwell.

Mohan, B. (1986). *Language and content.* Reading, MA: Addison-Wesley.

Mohan, B., & Beckett, G. H. (2001). A functional approach to research on content-based language learning: Recasts in causal explanations. *The Canadian Modern Language Review, 58,* 133–155.

Mori, H. (2000). Error treatment at different grade levels in Japanese immersion classroom interaction. *Studies in Language Sciences, 1,* 171–180.

Mori, H. (2002). *Error treatment sequences in Japanese immersion classroom interactions at different grade levels.* Unpublished doctoral dissertation, University of California, Los Angeles.

Mougeon, R., & Beniak, É. (1991). *Linguistic consequences of language contact and restriction: The case of French in Ontario, Canada.* Oxford: Oxford University Press.

Mougeon, R. & Rehner, K. (2001). Acquisition of sociolinguistic variants by French immersion students: The case of restrictive expressions, and more. *The Modern Language Journal, 85,* 398–415.

Muranoi, H. (2000). Focus on form through interaction enhancement: Integrating formal instruction into a communicative task in EFL classrooms. *Language Learning, 50,* 617–673.

Muñoz, C. (2007). Age-related differences and second language learning practice. In R. DeKeyser (Ed.), *Practicing for second language use: Perspectives from applied linguistics and cognitive psychology* (pp. 229–255). Cambridge, UK: Cambridge University Press.

Murphy, V. (2000). Compounding and the representation of L2 inflectional morphology. *Language Learning, 50,* 153–197.

Musumeci, D. (1996). Teacher-learner negotiation in content-based instruction: Communication at cross-purposes? *Applied Linguistics, 17,* 286–325.

Nadasdi, T., Mougeon, R., & Rehner, K. (2005). Learning to speak everyday (Canadian) French. *The Canadian Modern Language Review, 61,* 543–564.

Nassaji, H., & Wells, G. (2000). What's the use of 'triadic dialogue'?: An investigation of teacher-student interaction. *Applied Linguistics, 21,* 376–406.

Naughton, D. (2006). Cooperative strategy training and oral interaction: Enhancing small group communication in the language classroom. *The Modern Language Journal, 90,* 169–184.

Netten, J. (1991). Towards a more language oriented second language classroom. In L. Malavé & G. Duquette (Eds.), *Language, culture and cognition* (pp. 284–304). Clevedon, UK: Multilingual Matters.

Netten, J. & Spain, W. (1989). Student-teacher interaction patterns in the French immersion classroom: Implications for levels of achievement in French language proficiency. *The Canadian Modern Language Review, 45,* 485–501.

Nicholas, H., Lightbown, P., & Spada, N. (2001). Recasts as feedback to language learners. *Language Learning, 51,* 719–758.

Nunan, D. (1989). *Designing tasks for the communicative classroom.* Cambridge, UK: Cambridge University Press.

Nuttall, C., & Langhan, D. (1998). The Molteno Project: A case study of immersion for English-medium instruction in South Africa. In K. Johnson & M. Swain (Eds.), *Immersion education: International perspectives* (pp. 210–238). Cambridge, UK: Cambridge University Press.

Norris, J. & Ortega, L. (2000). Effectiveness of L2 instruction: A research synthesis and quantitative meta-analysis. *Language Learning, 50,* 417–528.

Oladejo, J. (1993). Error correction in ESL: Learners' preferences. *TESL Canada Journal, 10,* 71–89.

Oliver, R. (1995). Negative feedback in child NS-NNS conversation. *Studies in Second Language Acquisition, 17,* 459–481.

Oliver, R., & Mackey, A. (2003). Interactional context and feedback in child ESL classrooms. *The Modern Language Journal, 87,* 519–533.

O'Malley, M., & Chamot, A. (1990). *Learning strategies in second language acquisition.* Cambridge, UK: Cambridge University Press.

Ouellet, M. (1990). *Synthèse historique de l'immersion française au Canada suivie d'une bibliographie sélective et analytique.* Quebec City, QC: Centre international de recherche sur le bilinguisme.

Pally, M. (Ed.). (2000). *Sustained content teaching in academic ESL/EFL.* Boston/New York: Houghton Mifflin.

Panova, I., & Lyster, R. (2002). Patterns of feedback and uptake in an adult ESL classroom. *TESOL Quarterly, 36,* 573–595.

Peal, E., & Lambert, W. (1962). The relation of bilingualism to intelligence. *Psychological Monographs, 76,* 1–23.

Peritz, I. (2006). 'Language bath' parents earn a merci beaucoup. Bell Globemedia Publishing (March 22).

Petit, J. (2002). Acquisition strategies of German in Alsation immersion classrooms. In P. Burmeister, T. Piske, & A. Rohde (Eds.), *An integrated view of language development: Papers in Honor of Henning Wode* (pp. 433–448). Trier, Germany: Wissenschaftlicher Verlag Trier.

Philp, J. (2003). Constraints on "noticing the gap": Nonnative speakers' noticing of recasts in NS-NNS interaction. *Studies in Second Language Acquisition, 25,* 99–126.

Pica, T. (1994). Research on negotiation: What does it reveal about second-language learning conditions, processes, and outcomes? *Language Learning, 44,* 493–527.

Pica, T. (2000). Tradition and transition in English language teaching methodology. *System, 28,* 1–18.

Pica, T. (2002). Subject-matter content: How does it assist the interactional and linguistic needs of classroom language learners? *The Modern Language Journal, 86,* 1–19.

Pica, T., Holliday, L., Lewis, N., & Morgenthaler, L. (1989). Comprehensible output as an outcome of linguistic demands on the learner. *Studies in Second Language Acquisition, 11,* 63–90.

Pica, T., Kanagy, R., & Falodun, J. (1993). Choosing and using communication tasks for second language instruction and research. In G. Crookes & S. Gass (Eds.), *Tasks and language learning: Integrating theory and practice* (pp. 9–34). Clevedon, UK: Multilingual Matters.

Pica, T., Kang, H.-S., & Sauro, S. (2006). Information gap tasks: Their multiple roles and contributions to interaction research methodology. *Studies in Second Language Acquisition, 28*, 301–338.

Pica, T., Lincoln-Porter, F., Paninos, D., & Linnell, J. (1996). Language learners' interaction: How does it address the input, output, and feedback needs of L2 learners? *TESOL Quarterly, 30*, 59–84.

Pica, T., Young, R., & Doughty, C. (1987). The impact of interaction on comprehension. *TESOL Quarterly, 21*, 737–758.

Ranta, L. (2002). The role of learners' language analytic ability in the communicative classroom. In P. Robinson (Ed.), *Individual differences and instructed language learning* (pp. 159–180). Amsterdam/Philadelphia: John Benjamins.

Ranta, L., & Lyster, R. (2007). A cognitive approach to improving immersion students' oral language abilities: The Awareness-Practice-Feedback sequence. In R. DeKeyser (Ed.), *Practicing for second language use: Perspectives from applied linguistics and cognitive psychology* (pp. 141–160). Cambridge, UK: Cambridge University Press.

Rebuffot, J. (1993). *Le point sur l'immersion au Canada.* Montreal, QC: Éditions CEC.

Rebuffot, J. (1998). Aspects récents de l'immersion en français au Canada: vers le renouvellement de la pédagogie immersive. In J. Arnau & J. Artigal (Eds.), *Immersion programmes: A European perspective* (pp. 685–692). Barcelona: Publicacions de la Universitat de Barcelona.

Rebuffot, J., & Lyster, R. (1996). L'immersion au Canada: contextes, effets et pédagogie. In J. Erfurt (Ed.), *De la polyphonie à la symphonie. Méthodes, théories et faits de la recherche pluridisciplinaire sur le français au Canada* (pp. 277–294). Leipzig: Leipziger Universitätsverlag GmbH.

Rehner, K., & Mougeon, R. (1999) Variation in the spoken French of immersion students: To 'ne' or not to 'ne,' that is the sociolinguistic question. *The Canadian Modern Language Review, 56*, 124–154.

Riches, C. (2001). *The development of L1 and L2 reading in two bilingual education contexts.* Unpublished doctoral dissertation, McGill University, Montreal, Canada.

Roberts, M. (1995). Awareness and the efficacy of error correction. In R. Schmidt (Ed.), *Attention and awareness in foreign language learning* (Tech. Rep. No. 9) (pp. 162–182). Honolulu, HI: University of Hawai'i, Second Language Teaching and Curriculum Center.

Robinson, P., & Ha, M. (1993). Instance theory and second language rule learning under explicit conditions. *Studies in Second Language Acquisition, 13*, 413–438.

Rodgers, D. (2006). Developing content and form: Encouraging evidence from Italian content-based instruction. *The Modern Language Journal, 90*, 373–386.

Rutherford, W. (1987). *Second language grammar: Learning and teaching.* London: Longman.

Salomone, A. (1992a). Immersion teachers' pedagogical beliefs and practices: Results of a descriptive analysis. In E. Bernhardt (Ed.), *Life in language immersion classrooms* (pp. 9–44). Clevedon, UK: Multilingual Matters.

Salomone, A. (1992b). Student-teacher interactions in selected French immersion classrooms. In E. Bernhardt (Ed.), *Life in language immersion classrooms* (pp. 97–109). Clevedon, UK: Multilingual Matters.

Samuda, V. (2001). Guiding relationships between form and meaning during task performance: The role of the teacher. In M. Bygate, P. Skehan, & M. Swain (Eds.), *Researching pedagogic tasks: Second language learning, teaching and testing* (pp. 119–140). Harlow, UK: Pearson Education.

Sato, M., & Lyster, R. (in press). Modified output of Japanese EFL learners: Variable effects of interlocutor vs. feedback types. In A. Mackey (Ed.), *Conversational interaction in second language acquisition: A series of empirical studies*. Oxford: Oxford University Press.

Schachter, J. (1983). Nutritional needs of language learners. In M. Clarke & J. Handscombe (Eds.), *On TESOL '82: Pacific perspectives on learning and teaching* (pp. 175–189). Washington, DC: TESOL.

Schegloff, E., Jefferson, G., & Sacks, H. (1977). The preference for self-correction in the organization of repair in conversation. *Language, 53,* 361–382.

Schleppegrell, M., Achugar, M., & Orteíza, T. (2004). The grammar of history: Enhancing content-based instruction through a functional focus on language. *TESOL Quarterly, 38,* 67–93.

Schmidt, R. (1990). The role of consciousness in second language learning. *Applied Linguistics, 11,* 129–158.

Schmidt, R. (1992). Psychological mechanisms underlying second language fluency. *Studies in Second Language Acquisition, 14,* 357–385.

Schmidt, R. (1993). Consciousness, learning and interlanguage pragmatics. In G. Kasper & S. Blum-Kulka (Eds.), *Interlanguage pragmatics* (pp. 21–41). Oxford: Oxford University Press.

Schmidt, R. (1994). Deconstructing consciousness in search of useful definitions for applied linguistics. *AILA Review, 11,* 11–26.

Schulz, R. (1996). Focus on form in the foreign language classroom: Students' and teachers' views on error correction and the role of grammar. *Foreign Language Annals, 29,* 343–364.

Schulz, R. (2001). Cultural differences in student and teacher perceptions concerning the role of grammar instruction and corrective feedback: USA-Columbia. *The Modern Language Journal, 85,* 244–258.

Schwartz, B. (1993). On explicit and negative data effecting and affecting competence and linguistic behaviour. *Studies in Second Language Acquisition, 15,* 147–164.

Seedhouse, P. (2004). *The interactional architecture of the language classroom: A conversation analysis perspective.* Malden, MA: Blackwell.

Segalowitz, N. (1997). Individual differences in second language acquisition. In A. de Groot & J. Kroll (Eds.), *Tutorials in bilingualism: Psycholinguistic perspectives* (pp. 85–112). Mahwah, NJ: Lawrence Erlbaum.

Segalowitz, N. (2000). Automaticity and attentional skill in fluent performance. In H. Riggenbach (Ed.), *Perspectives on fluency* (pp. 200–219). Ann Arbor, MI: University of Michigan Press.

Segalowitz, N. (2003). Automaticity and second language learning. In C. Doughty & M. Long (Eds.), *Handbook of second language acquisition* (pp. 382–408). Oxford: Blackwell.

Selinker, L., Swain, M., & Dumas, G. (1975). The interlanguage hypothesis extended to children. *Language Learning, 25,* 139–152.

Sharwood Smith, M. (1981). Consciousness-raising and the second language learner. *Applied Linguistics, 2,* 159–168.

Sharwood Smith, M. (1993). Input enhancement in instructed SLA. *Studies in Second Language Acquisition, 15,* 165–179.

Sheen, Y. (2004) Corrective feedback and learner uptake in communicative classrooms across instructional settings. *Language Teaching Research, 8,* 263–300.

Sheen, Y. (in press). The effect of focused written corrective feedback and language aptitude on ESL learners' acquisition of articles. *TESOL Quarterly 42,* 2.

Shehadeh, A. (1999). Non-native speakers' production of modified comprehensible output and second language learning. *Language Learning, 49,* 627–675.

Shehadeh, A. (2001). Self- and other-initiated modified output during task-based interaction. *TESOL Quarterly, 35,* 433–457.

Shehadeh, A. (2003). Learner output, hypothesis testing, and internalizing linguistic knowledge. *System, 31,* 155–171.

Shiffrin, R. M., & Schneider, W. (1977). Controlled and automatic human information processing: II. Perceptual learning, automatic attending, and a general theory. *Psychological Review, 84,* 127–190.

Short, D. (1994). Expanding middle school horizons: Integrating language, culture, and social studies. *TESOL Quarterly, 28,* 581–608.

Short, D. (2002). Language learning in sheltered social studies classes. *TESOL Journal, 11,* 18–24.

Sinclair, J., & Coulthard, R. M. (1975). *Towards an analysis of discourse: The English used by teachers and pupils.* Oxford: Oxford University Press.

Singh, R. (1986). Immersion: problems and principles. *The Canadian Modern Language Review, 42,* 559–571

Skehan, P. (1998). *A cognitive approach to language learning.* Oxford: Oxford University Press.

Slaughter, H. (1997). Indigenous language immersion in Hawai'i: A case study of Kula Kaiapuni Hawai'I, an effort to save the indigenous language of Hawai'i. In K. Johnson & M. Swain (Eds.), *Immersion education: International perspectives* (pp. 105–130). Cambridge, UK: Cambridge University Press.

Slimani, A. (1992). Evaluation of classroom interaction. In C. Anderson & A. Beretta (Eds.), *Evaluating second language education* (pp. 197–221). Cambridge, UK: Cambridge University Press.

Smith, N., & Shapson, S. (1999). Transformative teaching: An agenda for faculties of education. *Education Canada, 39* (1), 4–8.

Snow, M. (1987). *Immersion teacher handbook.* Los Angeles: UCLA.

Snow, M., Met, M., & Genesee, F. (1989). A conceptual framework for the integration of language and content in second/foreign language instruction. *TESOL Quarterly, 23,* 201–217.

Spada, N. (1997). Form-focussed instruction and second language acquisition: A review of classroom and laboratory research. *Language Teaching, 29,* 73–87.

Spada, N. & Fröhlich, M. (1995). *COLT. Communicative Orientation of Language Teaching observation scheme: Coding conventions and applications.* Sydney, Australia: National Centre for English Language Teaching and Research.

Spada, N., & Lightbown, P. M. (1993). Instruction and the development of questions in L2 classrooms. *Studies in Second Language Acquisition, 15,* 205–224.

Spada, N., & Lightbown, P. M. (1999). Instruction, first language influence, and developmental readiness in second language acquisition. *The Modern Language Journal, 83,* 1–22.

Spada, N., Lightbown, P. M., & White, J. (2005). The importance of form/meaning mappings in explicit form-focused instruction. In A. Housen & M. Pierrard (Eds.), *Investigations in instructed second language acquisition* (pp. 199–234). Amsterdam: Mouton de Gruyter.

Stern, H. H. (1990). Analysis and experience as variables in second language pedagogy. In B. Harley, P. Allen, J. Cummins, & M. Swain (Eds.), *The development of second language proficiency* (pp. 93–109). Cambridge, UK: Cambridge University Press.

Stern, H. H. (1992). *Issues and options in language teaching.* Oxford: Oxford University Press.

Stigler, J., & Hiebert, J. (1999). *The teaching gap: Best ideas from the world's teachers for improving education in the classroom.* New York: The Free Press.

Storch, N. (2002). Patterns of interaction in ESL pair work. *Language Learning, 52,* 119–158.

Swain, M. (1985). Communicative competence: Some roles of comprehensible input and comprehensible output in its development In S. Gass & C. Madden (Eds.), *Input in second language acquisition* (pp. 235–253). Rowley, MA: Newbury House.

Swain, M. (1988). Manipulating and complementing content teaching to maximize second language learning. *TESL Canada Journal, 6,* 68–83.

Swain, M. (1993). The Output Hypothesis: Just speaking and writing aren't enough. *The Canadian Modern Language Review, 50,* 158–165.

Swain, M. (1995). Three functions of output in second language learning. In G. Cook & B. Seidlhofer (Eds.), *Principle and practice in applied linguistics: Studies in honour of H. G. Widdowson* (pp. 125–144). Oxford: Oxford University Press.

Swain, M. (1996). Integrating language and content in immersion classrooms: research perspectives. *The Canadian Modern Language Review, 52,* 529–548.

Swain, M. (1998). Focus on form through conscious reflection. In C. Doughty & J. Williams (Eds.), *Focus on form in classroom second language acquisition* (pp. 64–81). Cambridge, UK: Cambridge University Press.

Swain, M. (2000). French immersion research in Canada: Recent contributions to SLA and Applied Linguistics. *Annual Review of Applied Linguistics, 20,* 199–212.

Swain, M. (2005). The output hypothesis: Theory and research. In E. Hinkel (Ed.), *Handbook of research in second language teaching and learning* (pp. 471–484). Mahwah, NJ: Lawrence Erlbaum.

Swain, M., & Carroll, S. (1987). The immersion observation study. In B. Harley, P. Allen, J. Cummins, & M. Swain (Eds.), *Development of bilingual proficiency. Final report. Volume II: Classroom treatment* (pp. 190–316). Toronto, ON: Modern Language Centre, OISE/UT.

Swain M, & Johnson, K. (1997). Immersion education: A category within bilingual education. In K. Johnson & M. Swain M (Eds.), *Immersion education: International perspectives* (pp. 1–16). Cambridge, UK: Cambridge University Press.

Swain, M., & Lapkin, S. (1982). *Evaluating bilingual education in Ontario: A Canadian case study.* Clevedon, UK: Multilingual Matters.

Swain, M. & Lapkin, S. (1990). Aspects of the sociolinguistic performance of early and late French immersion students. In R. Scarcella, E. Andersen, & S. Krashen (Eds.), *Developing communicative competence in a second language* (pp. 41–54). New York: Newbury House.

Swain, M. & Lapkin, S. (1995). Problems in output and the cognitive processes they generate: A step towards second language learning. *Applied Linguistics, 16,* 370–391.

Swain, M., & Lapkin, S. (1998). Interaction and second language learning: Two adolescent French immersion students working together. *The Modern Language Journal, 82,* 320–37.

Swain, M., & Lapkin, S. (2000). Task-based second language learning: The uses of the first language. *Language Teaching Research, 4,* 253–276.

Swain, M., & Lapkin, S. (2001). Focus on form through collaborative dialogue: Exploring task effects. In M. Bygate, P. Skehan, & M. Swain (Eds.), *Researching pedagogic tasks: Second language learning, teaching and testing* (pp. 99–118). Harlow, UK: Pearson Education.

Swain, M., & Lapkin, S. (2002). Talking it through: Two French immersion learners' response to reformulation. *International Journal of Educational Research, 37,* 285–304.

Swain, M., & Lapkin, S. (2005). The evolving sociopolitical context of immersion education in Canada: Some implications for program development. *International Journal of Applied Linguistics, 15,* 169–186.

Tardif, C. (1991). Quelques traits distinctifs de la pédagogie d'immersion. *Études de linguistique appliquée, 82,* 39–51.

Tardif, C. (1994). Classroom teacher talk in early immersion. *The Canadian Modern Language Review, 50,* 466–481.

Tarone, E. & Swain, M. (1995). A sociolinguistic perspective on second-language use in immersion classrooms. *The Modern Language Journal, 79,* 166–178.

Tharpe, R., & Gallimore, R. (1988). *Rousing minds to life: Teaching, learning, and schooling in social context.* New York: Cambridge University Press.

Tomlin, R., & Villa, V. (1994). Attention in cognitive science and second language acquisition. *Studies in Second Language Acquisition, 16,* 183–203.

Tourond, M. (1982). *Tests diagnostiques de lecture.* Toronto, ON: OISE Press.

Towell, R. & Hawkins, R. (1994). *Approaches to second language acquisition.* Clevedon, UK: Multilingual Matters.

Trahey, M., & White, L. (1993). Positive evidence and preemption in the second language classroom. *Studies in Second Language Acquisition, 15,* 181–204.

Truscott, J. (1999). What's wrong with oral grammar correction. *The Canadian Modern Language Review, 55,* 437–456.

Tsang, W. (2004). Feedback and uptake in teacher-student interaction: An analysis of 18 English lessons in Hong Kong secondary classrooms. *Regional Language Centre Journal, 35,* 187–209.

Tucker, R., Lambert, W. E., & Rigault, A. (1977). *The French speaker's skill with grammatical gender: An example of rule-governed behaviour.* Paris: Mouton.

Turnbull, M. (2001). There is a role for the L1 in second and foreign language teaching, but... *The Canadian Modern Language Review, 57,* 531–540.

Turnbull, M., & Arnett, K. (2002). Teachers' uses of the target and first languages in second and foreign language classrooms. *Annual Review of Applied Linguistics, 22,* 204–218.

Turnbull, M., Lapkin, S., & Hart, D. (2001). Grade 3 immersion students' performance in literacy and mathematics: Province-wide results from Ontario (1989–1999). *The Canadian Modern Language Review, 58,* 9–26.

Turnbull, M., Lapkin, S., Hart, D., & Swain, M. (1998). Time on task and immersion graduates' French proficiency. In S. Lapkin (Ed.), *French second language education in Canada: Empirical studies* (pp. 31–55). Toronto, ON: University of Toronto Press.

Van den Branden, K. (1997). Effects of negotiation on language learners' output. *Language Learning, 47,* 589–636.

van Lier, L. (1988). *The classroom and the language learner.* London: Longman.

VanPatten, B. (1990). Attending to content and form in the input: An experiment in consciousness. *Studies in Second Language Acquisition, 12,* 287–301.

VanPatten, B. (1996). *Input processing and grammar instruction: Theory and research.* Norwood, NJ: Ablex.

VanPatten, B. (Ed.). (2004). *Processing instruction: Theory, research, and commentary.* Mahwah, NJ: Lawrence Erlbaum.

Varonis, E., & Gass, S. (1985). Non-native/non-native conversations: A model for negotiation of meaning. *Applied Linguistics, 6,* 71–90.

Vigil, N., & Oller, J. (1976). Rule fossilization: A tentative model. *Language Learning, 26,* 281–295.

Vygotsky, L. S. (1978). *Mind in society: The development of higher psychological processes.* Cambridge, MA: Harvard University Press.

Wajnryb, R. (1990). *Grammar dictation.* Oxford: Oxford University Press.

Warden, M., Lapkin, S., Swain, M., & Hart, D. (1995). Adolescent language learners on a three-month exchange: Insights from their diaries. *Foreign Language Annals, 28,* 537–550.

Weber, S., & Tardif, C. (1991). Assessing L2 competency in early immersion classrooms. *The Canadian Modern Language Review, 47,* 916–932.

Weiner, S. L., & Goodenough, D. R. (1977). A move toward a psychology of conversation. In R. Freedle (Ed.), *Discourse production and comprehension* (pp. 213–225). Norwood, NJ: Ablex.

Wells, G. (2001). The development of a community of inquirers. In G. Wells (Ed.), *Action, talk, and text: Learning and teaching through inquiry* (pp. 1–22). New York: Teachers College Press.

Wesche, M. (1993). French immersion graduates at university and beyond: What difference has it made? In J. Alatis (Ed.), *Georgetown University Round Table on Languages and Linguistics 1992: Language, communication and social meaning* (pp. 208–240). Washington, DC: Georgetown University Press.

Wesche, M. (2002). Early French immersion: How has the original Canadian model stood the test of time? In P. Burmeister, T. Piske, & A. Rohde (Eds.), *An integrated view of language development: Papers in honor of Henning Wode* (pp. 357–375). Trier, Germany: Wissenschaftlicher Verlag Trier.

Wesche, M., & Skehan, P. (2002). Communicative, task-based, and content-based language instruction. In R. Kaplan, (Ed.), *The Oxford handbook of applied linguistics* (pp. 207–228). Oxford: Oxford University Press.

White, J. (1998). Getting the learners' attention: A typographical input enhancement study. In C. Doughty & J. Williams (Eds.), *Focus on form in classroom second language acquisition* (pp. 85–113). Cambridge, UK: Cambridge University Press.

White, J., & Ranta, L. (2002). Examining the interface between metalinguistic task performance and oral production in a second language. *Language Awareness, 11,* 259–290.

White, L. (1991). Argument structure in second language acquisition. *Journal of French Language Studies, 1,* 189–207.

Williams, J. (1999). Learner-generated attention to form. *Language Learning, 49,* 583–625.

Williams, J., & Evans, J. (1998). What kind of focus and on which forms? In C. Doughty & J. Williams (Eds.), *Focus on form in classroom second language acquisition* (pp. 139–155). Cambridge, UK: Cambridge University Press.

Williams, M. & Burden, R. (1997). *Psychology for language teachers: A social constructivist approach.* Cambridge, UK: Cambridge University Press.

Willis, J. (1996). *A framework for task-based learning.* Harlow, UK: Addison Wesley Longman.

Wood, D., Bruner, J., & Ross, G. (1976). The role of tutoring in problem solving. *Journal of Child Psychology and Psychiatry, 17,* 89–100.

Wright, R. (1996). A study of the acquisition of verbs of motion by grade 4/5 early French immersion students. *The Canadian Modern Language Review, 53,* 257–280.

Yamauchi, L., & Wilhelm, P. (2001). *Ola Ka Hawai'i I Kona 'Ōlelo*: Hawaiians live in their language. In D. Christian & F. Genesee (Eds.), *Bilingual education* (pp. 83–94). Alexandria, VA: TESOL.

Author index

Subject index

In the series *Language Learning & Language Teaching* the following titles have been published thus far or are scheduled for publication: